Transpersonal Development

Cultivating the Human Resources of Peace, Wisdom, Purpose and Oneness

Richard Schaub, PhD
Bonney Gulino Schaub, RN, MS, PMHCNS-BC

Foreword by Larry Dossey, MD

Florence Press

ISBN: 9780615622415
Copyright © 2013 Richard Schaub PhD

By Richard Schaub, PhD & Bonney Gulino Schaub, RN, MS, PMHCNS-BC

2 Murray Court
Huntington NY 11743
631.673.0293
drrichardschaub@gmail.com
www.huntingtonmeditation.com

Cover artwork by Grace Califano Schaub
Book design by Dean Whitney, Aericon.com

For Fiona, Ava,

Lucie and Marisol

Table of Contents

List of Practices

Foreword
by Larry Dossey, MD

"As Mind at Large seeps past the no longer watertight valve [of the brain], all kinds of biologically useless things start to happen. In some cases there may be extra-sensory perceptions. Other persons discover a world of visionary beauty. To others again is revealed the glory, the infinite value and meaningfulness of naked existence, of the given, unconceptualized event. In the final stage of egolessness there is an 'obscure knowledge' that All is in all — that All is actually each." — ALDOUS HUXLEY[1]

During the twentieth century our concept of consciousness underwent considerable refinement. We were introduced to several subdivisions of consciousness — the preconscious, the subconscious, the unconscious, the collective conscious, and the collective unconscious. It has become increasingly clear to many that an additional category of consciousness is required in order to accommodate a certain type of experience that has been largely ignored by conventional psychology. This addition to the typology of consciousness is transpersonal consciousness or transpersonal awareness.

What is a transpersonal experience? In *Transpersonal Development,* authors Bonney and Richard Schaub provide many examples from their clinical practice. They describe the four main qualities of these experiences — a sense of peace, wisdom, purpose and oneness. They explain why transpersonal experiences are a feature of a mature, healthy psyche, and they instruct us how to access the transpersonal domain.

Psychologists often devote their entire career to helping patients develop a healthy ego and a strong personality. While this goal is laudable, many clients, as the Schaubs describe, having achieved this level of psychological maturity find themselves asking, "Is this all there is?" *Transpersonal Development* answers, "There is more; there are higher levels of consciousness lying beyond the personality and sense of self."

This does not mean that conventional psychology is somehow wrong, but that it is incomplete. Conventional psychology is related to transpersonal psychology, as classical physics is related to quantum/relativistic physics. For three centuries it was believed that Sir Isaac Newton's laws of motion could adequately describe everything that occurred in the physical world. The classical tenets are well known. Space and time were considered absolutes; time was believed to be linear, flowing in one direction; nothing happened without a cause; and a cause always preceded an effect. But as the nineteenth century transitioned to the twentieth, exceptions to Newton's certainties were encountered. With Planck's discovery of the quantum and Einstein's elaboration of his special theory of relativity, the classical worldview changed forever. When events involving galactic distances and near light-speed were scrutinized, Newton's laws broke down. Subatomic events were found to behave randomly and could be uncaused. Space and time were no longer considered absolute, but relative. As the speed of an object approached the speed of light, time slowed and its mass expanded. Physical objects that appeared solid were shown to be almost totally comprised of empty space. This new view of the world violated common sense, for there were no obvious analogies in daily experience that might corroborate it. Still, quantum/relativistic physics did not demolish classical physics. Newton's principles still work well in everyday life: we can predict eclipses, chart the course of comets, and put humans on the moon using them. But classical physics is radically incomplete and inadequate in other situations. Put simply, it cannot account for what we observe.

Just so, although conventional psychology is effective in addressing the anxieties and upsets most of us face as we go about our lives, there are exceptional, majestic experiences that require another perspective. This is where transpersonal psychology enters, and this is what *Transpersonal Development* is all about.

The sense of oneness that is a feature of transpersonal experiences deserves emphasis. We commonly believe that human minds are individual, one mind per person, around seven billion separate minds on the planet. Yet a considerable body of evidence suggests that view is incomplete. Today there are scores of studies that demonstrate that individuals can *acquire* information from the environment remotely, at a distance, beyond the reach of the physical senses; and that individuals can *insert* information into the environment remotely as well. The view of consciousness that is emerging from these findings is that it is *nonlocal* — i.e., not localized or confined to specific locations in space, such as the brain and body, nor localized or confined to specific points in time, such as the present. This means that consciousness is unbounded, so that in some dimension all minds must come together to form a unified, single consciousness I've called the One Mind. This is an ancient concept, traceable to previous millennia in several cultures. What is different in our day is the empirical evidence supporting such a view.[2]

The relevance to transpersonal development is straightforward. As the Schaubs describe, a sense of oneness, unity, and unbroken wholeness is a universal, distinguishing characteristic of transpersonal experiences. This is often accompanied by a sense of joy and fulfillment, and the feeling that the world is being sensed the way it really is, an unbroken whole. During such moments, the separateness of minds is often felt to be an illusion.

The skeptical response frequently is that such experiences are illusions, but such skepticism too often denies the unity that many scholars believe lies at the heart of the world. Some of the greatest scientists of the twentieth century believed that the wholeness that is sensed in transpersonal moments goes beyond the physical world to involve consciousness itself. This includes Nobel physicist Erwin Schrödinger, who proclaimed, "Mind is by its very nature a *singulare tantum*. I should say: the overall number of minds is just one."[3] And the distinguished physicist David Bohm asserted, "Deep down the consciousness of mankind is one. This is a virtual certainty… and if we don't see this it's because we are blinding ourselves to it."[4]

What about the other qualities of transpersonal experience the Schaubs describe — peace, wisdom, and purpose? These follow from the oneness and wholeness of consciousness. For if the principle of oneness is valid, then individual consciousness has access to the greater consciousness, via the single, unitary, collective One Mind, as physicists Schrödinger and Bohm saw. The One mind becomes, then, a source of infinite wisdom, knowledge, and creativity, with the attendant features of peace and purpose.

Creative individuals occasionally dip into this reservoir of wisdom and creativity, and some leave descriptions of the experience. This includes Thomas Edison, America's great inventor, who summed up his experience thus: «People say I have created things. I have never created anything. I get impressions from the Universe at large and work them out, but I am only a plate on a record or a receiving apparatus — what you will. Thoughts are really impressions that we get from outside.»[5] The eminent German physicist and philosopher Baron Carl Friedrich von Weizsäcker agreed: "[In any great discovery] we find the often disturbing and happy experience: 'It is not I; I have not done this.' Still, in a certain way it is I — yet not the ego ...but...a more comprehensive self."[6]

In addition to implying an infinite source of wisdom and creativity via unitary consciousness, the nonlocal perspective also implies infinitude in time for some aspect of conscious-ness. "Infinitude in time" is a fancy term for immortality. Thus the transpersonal perspective has the possibility to allay the fear of annihilation with physical death. This contribu-tion is seismic, because the fear of death has probably caused more suffering in human history than all the physical diseases combined.

I hope it is clear that the transpersonal view is not a philo-sophical plaything, but a perspective that is required by both widespread human experience and empirical findings, and which has the potential to revolutionize the dismal, modern view of our origins and destiny. The transpersonal view advo-cated by the Schaubs, therefore, is not "just psychology" but a potentially world-changing perspective. This recognition is timely. As part of a larger consciousness, we have access to all possible wisdom and creativity, which we sorely need if we are to confront the many challenges we face as humans on a fragile planet.

Bonney and Richard Schaub have accomplished something rare. You will probably never encounter a treatise on transper-sonal development with the depth, brevity, and clarity of this book. It is an honor to recommend it.

~ Larry Dossey, MD

REFERENCES

[1] Aldous Huxley. *The Doors of Perception*. London, UK: Chatto and Windus; 1954. Reprint edition: London, UK: Granada Publishing; 1984: 22.

[2] Larry Dossey. *One Mind: How Our Individual Mind Is Part of a Greater Consciousness, and Why It Matters*. Carlsbad, CA: Hay House; 2013.

[3] Erwin Schrödinger. *What is Life? and Mind and Matter.* London, UK: Cambridge University Press; 1969: 145.

[4] David Bohm. Quoted in: Renée Weber. *Dialogues with Scientists and Sages*. New York, NY: Routledge & Kegan Paul; 1986: 41.

[5] Thomas Alva Edison. Quoted in: Neil Baldwin, *Edison: Inventing the Century.* NY: Hyperion; 1995:376.

[6] C. F. von Weizsäcker. Introduction. Gopi Krishna. *The Biological Basis of Religion and Genius*. New York, NY: Harper and Row; 1972: 35-36.

Introduction

Maria sounded very down on the phone: "I'm feeling so sorry for myself. My hair is coming out again. I'm eating myself to death."

"Higher consciousness objectively exists. It is one of the primary experiences of living. "

—*ROBERTO ASSAGIOLI, MD*

After a year of remission from cancer, she had just resumed chemotherapy. Her doctor was advising an aggressive series of treatments in reaction to Maria's new symptoms. She was depressed and enraged that cancer was back in her life. When she'd first gotten ill, she'd studied meditation with Richard to calm herself. Now she was looking for something more.

Richard asked her to put the phone on speaker, sit back in her chair, and close her eyes. He then guided her through the practice of Awareness Itself (**Practice 13** in this book). When Richard finished, there was silence on the other end of the phone for about three minutes. Then Maria exclaimed, "Wow!"

Wow turned out to be this:

"I felt the awareness like an energy between my eyebrows. Then it became visual - a yellow light with a gold rim around it. The light was alive and got so bright I could hardly see. I became immersed in it. I was in the light. Then I realized I was standing on the edge of an abyss of light. I thought, *What the hell*, and I dove in. You know I'm afraid to swim. I dove in! It was fabulous. I feel completely different."

She paused a moment and then added, "This is what I need."

What did she need? What had just happened to her? In the midst of a cancer recurrence and facing more chemotherapy, hair loss, weakness and nausea, Maria went beyond the part of her that is suffering. She'd gone into the transpersonal part of her nature.

Transpersonal means *beyond the personality*. It refers to the innate creative and spiritual resources we all have. When you need help or are called upon to help someone else, these resources can make a crucial difference. This book offers you the principles and step-by-step techniques of transpersonal practice, backed up by many case stories and the latest scientific research. Our hope is that every helping professional learns how to do transpersonal work.

Transpersonal means *beyond the personality*. It refers to the innate creative and spiritual resources we all have.

The First Step

You can take the first step right now by asking yourself this question, "What do I make of Maria's experience? Real, fake? Fantasy, amazing, weird…?"

As you will see throughout the book, we judge transpersonal practice on its merits: does it work? Maria's immersion into the light quickly lifted her mood. She felt peaceful, and she felt inspired by the very fact that she could have such an experience. A better mood, peace, and inspiration are surely evidence that the experience had a real effect. What pill could do as well?

But let's go deeper. There are many mysteries around such an experience. The most immediate mystery is that **Practice 13** has **none of the suggestions** that Maria experienced. The practice simply asks you to direct your awareness to listening,

The practice simply asks you to direct your awareness to listening, and then to your body, your face, your mouth, your nostrils, your left eye, your right eye and, lastly, the space between your eyebrows.

and then to your body, your face, your mouth, your nostrils, your left eye, your right eye and, lastly, the space between your eyebrows. That's it. The immersion into the light happened completely on its own: its appearance was mysterious. It was also unpredictable: neither Maria nor Richard could have imagined that diving into an *abyss of light* was going to happen while they were on the phone.

One aspect of Maria's experience, however, is neither mysterious nor unpredictable: it was healing. We know with confidence that your transpersonal nature, your creative and spiritual resources, holds a healing process. This process can be discovered by the kinds of practices we describe in *Part Two: The Huntington Method*.

The Lineage

There is almost a sensual longing for communion with others who have a large vision. The immense fulfillment of the friendship between those engaged in furthering the evolution of consciousness has a quality impossible to describe.

—*PIERRE TEILHARD DE CHARDIN*

There is nothing new about transpersonal practice. People of all times and cultures have found ways to awaken the creative and spiritual resources in human nature. The world's religious and spiritual art, literature and music are filled with stories of transpersonal experiences, including Maria-like entries into the light.

Crossing over into the modern scientific world of healthcare, there is a lineage of earlier practitioners who saw the need to heal the split between spirituality and science and used the term transpersonal in their work. They include William James PhD, Carl Jung MD, Roberto Assagioli MD, and Viktor Frankl MD, among many others. Our work is inspired by each of them, and since 1978 we have brought transpersonal work into hospitals, clinics, rehabilitation centers, institute training, employee wellness programs, counseling and coaching.

We recently met a new group of professionals who may continue the lineage.

It was 8:30 a.m. at the Hilton Hotel in Manhattan. Outside, a blizzard that had started the night before was clogging the city streets. The hotel ballroom was packed with people who'd made it through the snow to attend our seminar, "The Impact of Spiritual Experiences on Health."

After our lecture
and guided
meditations, a
line of people
were waiting to
talk with us. In
that morning of
conversations, we
were struck by the
intensity of the
search going on in
many people.
The first three
people on line
were physicians.

After our lecture and guided meditations, a line of people were waiting to talk with us. In that morning of conversations, we were struck by the intensity of the search going on in many people.

The first three people on line were physicians. As they listened in on each other's comments, they realized they'd arrived at a similar place in their careers. The concepts of compassion fatigue and vicarious trauma, applied to healthcare professionals who get worn down dealing with human problems everyday, certainly described them. But their struggle was more than that.

They needed hope and inspiration. When they'd first entered medicine, it was a calling - now it was a job. They'd thought they were going to make healing discoveries - now they were using their energy to keep the office staff and payroll going. Something was missing from their work: there had to be *more*. When they heard our descriptions of spiritual/transpersonal experiences positively affecting people's health, they each thought to themselves, "That's what I want to do."

They wondered about the next step, and they joked, wistfully, that they should open a new practice together. The same desire for the next step was true for the fourth person on line, a psychiatric nurse at a Veterans Administration hospital. He'd been in combat in the Army and wanted to know how to help other returning veterans gain access to their spirituality. The fifth person was a mental health counselor who was a serious student of meditation and wanted to know how to introduce it to his teenage clients in recovery from drug abuse.

New practice...spirituality...meditation...the next step...more. We've met many fellow professionals on the same wave length. They're really seekers, both scientific and spiritual, but they hesitate to bring their transpersonal/spiritual side directly into their work. Sitting across from them in their clinic or office, their patient or client is waiting for them to do so, just as Maria was.

Hope, inspiration, healing - it's what we're all waiting for.

The Huntington Method

To teach you transpersonal work, we have organized it around the four qualities of your transpersonal nature. These qualities are peace, wisdom, purpose and oneness.

Peace. There is a depth of inner peace in you far beyond relaxation. Relaxing is good, of course, and it is usually achieved by slowing down and distracting yourself (TV, vacation, dining out) as the method.

Inner peace, however, is not accessed by distracting your mind but by focusing it. When your mind focuses on one thing, your entire physiology calms down (Benson, 1975). You feel a quietly pervading joy and physically begin to restore your nervous system.

Wisdom. You have a guiding inner wisdom that includes but goes beyond rational thinking. It is a very different experience than *thinking about something*. Instead, wisdom comes to you as a synthetic understanding accompanied by a feeling of surprise, relief, and new knowing (Assagioli, 1965).

Across time and cultures, this higher intelligence, higher self, or higher knowing has been honored and symbolized (Schaub & Schaub, 2003). As you gain more and more access to this resource inside you, you begin to realize that the wisdom has its own orientation: it is actually guiding you toward your third transpersonal resource – your life purpose.

Across time and cultures, this higher intelligence, higher self, or higher knowing has been honored and symbolized.

Purpose. As a member of creation, you have built into you an evolutionary drive to contribute to life. It is what people are feeling when they say they want their life to have meaning, to matter, to make a difference. And there is a quiet but persistent suffering when you don't respond to this natural drive for meaning (Frankl, 1997). A day-in, day-out life which is meaningless confuses and disrupts your brain and nervous system (Hanson, 2009). There is now evidence that a new sense of meaning is a biological event that causes health-giving shifts in the brain (Kohls et al., 2011).

Oneness. This is the transpersonal resource that requires the most explanation. Oneness is not typically a subject of discussion at your clinic or school or private practice.

Oneness refers to the part of your nature that is capable of uniting with the energy of the universe beyond the limits of your mind and body. This may sound abstract or ethereal, but oneness objectively exists (Assagioli, 1991; Newberg and D'Aquili, 2001) and can be verified through your own direct experience independent of any belief system or sect. It is a moment in which you go beyond your mind and body and merge into an energy field of radiant bliss: remember Maria's dive into the abyss of light. In that merging, which may last one second of clock time but feels eternal, awareness and bliss are all that exist. Afterwards, back again in the mind and body, many people have characterized the oneness experience as a *reunion*, a *going home*. In religious terms, this *reunion* is with God.

Oneness helps to heal the fears related to your vulnerability as a separate self trying to survive in an uncertain world. As one example, we've seen the fear of death disappear in seriously ill patients after an experience of their innate oneness. It is a profound reassurance that they, and all of us, are participating in something far greater than our limited ideas about reality.

The **Huntington Method** is our synthesis of concepts and practices for awakening these transpersonal qualities in you and, through your skills, in the people who ask for your help.

A Note about Language

We address the writing in this book to *you*, the health professional. The book can also be used by any seeker for their own inner development.

The *we* in this book is Bonney and Richard Schaub. We drop the *we* voice when we describe a specific individual experience of Bonney's or Richard's.

From this point, we will use the term *client* to refer to the patients, clients, students, employees, and congregants who ask for your help.

PART ONE:

Transpersonal Basics

The Pioneers of Transpersonal Work

The first use of transpersonal has been attributed to William James, the "father" of American psychology, in 1905. It was later used by two European psychiatrists, Roberto Assagioli in Florence and Carl Jung in Zurich (Schaub & Schaub, 2003, 2009). Assagioli and Jung had been doctors through World War One and World War Two and saw the urgent need in their patients to discover new paths to inner peace and resilience. The traditional path, religion, had lost its credibility. The deaths of fifteen million Europeans in World War One and the deaths of forty million Europeans in World War Two made belief in a protective God unsustainable.

Assagioli emphasized meditative awareness practices, and Jung the guiding wisdom of inner images. Their approach was later enhanced by psychiatrist Viktor Frankl in Vienna, who had survived a Nazi concentration camp and began to teach his patients the healing power of life purpose. They saw that the discovery of meditative awareness, guiding wisdom, and life purpose were antidotes to the fear, stress, anxiety and struggling lives they saw in their practices. This is still true today.

They saw that the discovery of meditative awareness, guiding wisdom, and life purpose were antidotes to the fear, stress, anxiety and struggling lives they saw in their practices. This is still true today.

Their early transpersonal efforts were expanded upon in America by Lawrence LeShan (mind-body medicine), Elmer Green (biofeedback and states of consciousness), Herbert

Benson (mantra meditation and the relaxation response), Larry Dossey (prayer and the nonlocal mind), Barbara Dossey, Susan Luck and Bonney Gulino Schaub (integrative nurse coaching), Jon Kabat-Zinn (stress reduction and mindfulness), Ken Wilber (psychospiritual theory), John Welwood (psychotherapy and mindfulness), and many others.

The early transpersonal pioneers inspired a synthesis of science and spirituality whose effectiveness is now verified everyday in medical centers, clinics, business organizations, treatment programs, schools, and private practices.

Transpersonal and Spiritual

A factor in all transpersonal work has been the inclusion of practices from the world's spiritual heritage (Schaub, 1995). Meditation, imagery, prayer, yoga, tai chi and other practices with spiritual origins are now a recognized part of mind-body medicine. The National Center for Complementary and Alternative Medicine of the National Institutes of Health advocates that health and wellness professionals should become "catalysts and guides" in teaching these practices to clients (NCCAM, 2011). Combinations of spiritual practices and health treatment have emerged, including meditation for preventing relapse into depression, yoga for low back pain, imagery for trauma reduction, and many others.

There has been, however, a hesitation on the part of health professionals to identify with spiritual work, even if they are drawn to it. We believe that the term *transpersonal* solves this problem in two ways:

(1) Spirituality has immediate associations with religion and religiosity. The term transpersonal simply means *beyond the personality* and is neutral in regards to spirituality and religion. We can focus on transpersonal discoveries as health-giving experiences without getting tangled up in spiritual and religious beliefs.

(2) Transpersonal is a more descriptive term. Spiritual implies non-physical, ethereal, otherworldly. Transpersonal is grounded in your actual nature and the inherent capacities of your mind, body and feelings. In a transpersonal experience, you go beyond your normal understanding of who you are and, at the same time, become more of who you are.

In a transpersonal experience, you go beyond your normal understanding of who you are and, at the same time, become more of who you are.

Despite these distinctions, we still find ourselves using the terms transpersonal and spiritual interchangeably in both this book and in our public teaching. This is simply practical. While we call our work *transpersonal,* we appreciate that *spiritual* is a more generally understood term for referring to the higher/deeper aspects of human nature.

The Transpersonal and the Health Professional

In teaching transpersonal work over long careers in healthcare and mental health, we have seen a variety of attitudes toward spiritually-derived practices (see, for example, Birnbaum, Birnbaum & Mayseless, 2008):

- Professionals who have no knowledge and no interest in such matters - and therefore do not encourage their clients to be interested;
- Professionals who are hostile toward anything that sounds "spiritual," believing it to be unscientific, escapist fantasy;
- Professionals who are sympathetic to spiritual needs but associate them with religion and feel that religion is outside of their professional territory;
- Professionals who have had transpersonal experiences themselves but feel reluctant to bring their personal knowledge into their work;
- Professionals who, in the spirit of scientific inquiry and personal curiosity, have actively explored their own transpersonal nature to see what benefits it holds;
- Professionals who become active in encouraging transpersonal discovery in their clients through offering meditation, mental imagery and other practices.

Since you are reading this book, you are clearly willing to explore the transpersonal. A few professional challenges are worth noting.

The Challenges of Transpersonal Work

It is not uncommon for professionals to offer answers to clients which the professionals themselves would never accept. Medications are routinely prescribed that no prescribing physician would take. Diets are suggested that the professional doesn't follow. Advice is given about marriage problems that didn't work in the professional's personal life. It can still be useful information, but the professional is not an embodiment of it.

Transpersonal development is different. *You can't offer **The Huntington Method** unless you practice it yourself.* You are guiding clients deeper into their nature. To be a guide on this journey, you have to know where you are taking them. Additionally, without personal experience of your own transpersonal nature, you won't be effective in communicating about it.

Effective communication also requires that you find the right terminology. Even though transpersonal work derives mostly from spiritual practices, your role as a health professional in a multi-cultural society means that you need to explain the ideas and practices in secular language. Your degree of explanation will differ depending on the client's individual needs. Some will want an extended explanation in order to satisfy their intellect and feel secure. Others will only want reassurance that the practices work.

Transpersonal work is the gradual integration of transpersonal resources – inner peace, guiding inner wisdom, life purpose, and oneness – into your client's daily life, and into your own.

Probably the greatest challenge, however, is the pace of transpersonal work. The practices cause some immediate results which will surprise and please your clients. That is good, of course, but the real benefits of transpersonal discovery take place over time. Transpersonal work is the gradual integration of transpersonal resources – inner peace, guiding inner wisdom, life purpose, and oneness – into your client's daily life, and into your own.

As with all new development, transpersonal development in people unfolds at their own individual pace. One child begins to read at age four, another not until age seven. At age ten, they are both reading at the same level. One client can have many transpersonal experiences but little development. Another can have one sudden instance of transpersonal discovery and be changed by it from that moment on. Part of your role is to help clients to get the most benefit they can out of their transpersonal resources and experiences.

Common Anxieties Shared by Client and Professional

Transpersonal work involves a mixture of talking with your client and guiding your client through clinical meditation practices. Talking is familiar enough, but entering into meditation and imagery experiences may be very new for the client. When any of us are asked to try something new in the presence of another person, it tends to bring up performance anxiety. It is a normal and typical reaction. It is not unusual for anxiety to blunt the initial effectiveness of one of the **Huntington Method** practices.

There are three classic forms of anxiety that come up in clients when they are asked to try meditation or imagery:

> *What if I can't do it right?* (performance anxiety)
> *What if nothing happens?* (fear of failure)
> *What if I go out of control?* (fear of the unknown)

Strikingly, you as the professional may have the same three anxieties in introducing meditation and imagery:

> *I won't guide the client correctly.* (performance anxiety)
> *I'll offer this new practice and nothing will happen.*
> (fear of failure)
> *What if they get too upset or have bad memories?*
> (fear of the unknown)

The client's anxieties can be worked with by offering the practices as "something we are trying together." It's an exploration, an experiment, to see if the practices are helpful. This kind of message is collaborative in spirit and takes some of the pressure off the client to meet some implicit expectation.

Your own performance anxiety and fear of failure have a straightforward resolution. The answer is many hours of training in clinical meditation practices until they become familiar and trustworthy experiences. We have trained hundreds of professionals internationally and have seen them progress from anxiety to enjoyment in bringing the transpersonal into their work.

As trainers of health professionals, we actually feel relieved when our students express worry about harming a client. It means they are thinking about the client first.

The fear of the unknown, especially in regard to the fear of a client being harmed, is a more complex concern. As trainers of health professionals, we actually feel relieved when our students express worry about harming a client. It means they are thinking about the client first. There are two sources of confidence in alleviating this fear of the unknown.

The first is that transpersonal development is a collaborative effort between you and your client. You will be coaching the client through a process, and he or she will be reporting the effects to you. As you go along, you will be making adjustments to the practices, pace and goals. You may decide to use different or modified practices or none at all in response to your client's experiences.

Done in this manner, the client will be properly cared for. This collaborative process reassures even the most vulnerable clients that their needs will be respected.

The second source of confidence in entering the meditative unknown with a client is the objective existence of transpersonal resources in each person. Rather than fear of the unknown, the meditative and imagery practices open clients to *not previously known* depths of peace, wisdom, purpose and oneness in their nature. It is always a privilege to participate in the surprise of clients when they report the positive results of their transpersonal work.

We appreciate that a majority of professionals work in settings framed by symptom-based diagnoses of pathology. Transpersonal resources are not a typical subject of conversation. In addition, they may seem irrelevant for a client who is too phobic to walk across a parking lot or who is in a rage over a cancer recurrence. Clients in such crises, however, are exactly the ones who need to access their transpersonal resources and are often the most open to them.

As you develop your transpersonal skills, the three professional anxieties will fade away. **Part Two** covers the specific practices that will lead you into the encouraging and inspiring work of transpersonal discovery.

When is Transpersonal Work the Right Direction to Take?

Transpersonal/spiritual experiences are a biological and psychological event which cause health-giving shifts in the brain (Kohls et al., 2011). It is speculated that the health-giving shift is the brain processing a *new meaning to life* brought on by the transpersonal experience.

We could argue that anyone can benefit from transpersonal work, *but transpersonal work becomes crucial when the suffering is coming from maturity, and a new meaning to life is needed to relieve that suffering.*

The maturity we are speaking of has nothing to do with age. You can meet mature 13 year olds and immature 80 year olds. Maturity is the moment you realize that you are a vulnerable and temporary citizen of this world. You realize that there are no exceptions, not even you, to the cycle of creation: birth, growth, decline, death.

You have intimations of this basic vulnerability when losses happen. A big goal turns into a big disappointment. Trust turns into betrayal. Health turns into illness. Connection turns into abandonment. And, most of all, when someone dies. Life suddenly becomes different than you thought it was. It becomes uncertain. In that moment of maturity, you become a seeker, seeking to find a way of inner strength to face the uncertainty built into life.

Sensitive people are especially attuned to the change, loss and vulnerability inherent in life. For them, even a sunset, which of course happens every day, has a tinge of melancholy because it represents the passing of time. They are moved by the change of the seasons, see into the loneliness of a child, feel a visceral pain at the thought of an animal suffering, worry about people faraway who they don't know. They are mature by disposition and would benefit greatly from discovering their transpersonal resources.

At the opposite pole to sensitivity, there are people who live in denial of reality. They run away from maturity. They want to believe the cycle of creation only happens to other people. They invent rituals and beliefs that will hopefully gain them an exemption from reality. It's understandable: who wants to contemplate our essential vulnerability in this world?

Maturity is the moment you do contemplate it and know it's real. In that moment, there is one solid, dependable answer for your suffering - living a life of purpose. Writing about her 24 year struggle with cancer, author Katherine Russell Rich wrote: "When I was told I was going to die, I was shredded to realize I hadn't made any real difference" (New York Times, 2012). In the face of the uncertainty which is part of life, the certainty of your purpose for being here is your dependable organizing principle. It gets you through difficult times and rallies your hope, courage, and creativity to engage with life. When purpose is stabilized in you, you don't turn away from the world, never turn away, no matter what.

Meaning and Purpose

Assessing the rehabilitation needs of hundreds of cardiac in-patients in a major medical center, Richard heard over and over again the plaintive question of *what am I doing with my life?* One man looked with disgust at the stack of business messages waiting for him to deal with once he was discharged from the hospital. "They mean nothing to me," he shouted, and then dramatically threw them across the floor.

A crisis of meaning does not need a crisis of illness to activate it. John Whitmore (2009), a pioneer of the executive coaching movement, quotes one of his clients: "I am managing a large and successful company...I have good health; I have a wonderful family...But still I am not certain what I am doing with my life" (Whitmore, 2009, p. 203).

Your first reaction might be to feel that there is something seriously missing in this client. *What's his problem? Why can't he be happy with the good fortune he has?* As a professional, however, you are trained to reserve your judgments and instead turn toward your client with curiosity to find out more.

What is it that is missing in this client? Well, he has already told us: "…I am not certain what I am doing with my life."

This uncertainty clearly does not refer to his day-to-day living. He is busy, successful, and surrounded by support. It is a deeper feeling about his life that is bothering him. There is something he is not doing, something he is not getting to. The actual source of the uncertainty, though, is unknown to him. It is unconscious, and he needs to bring it into consciousness. As you will see, one of the skills of transpersonal development is to be able to guide clients deeper into their nature so that the unconscious becomes conscious.

It is understandable that our business executive doesn't know about the root of his uncertainty. Within the social definitions of goals in life, he should be a very happy man.

The Mid-Life Crisis

But he isn't happy. He doesn't know what he's doing with himself. He is a classic example of someone in mid-life who is in crisis. It has been made into a joke - the mid-life crisis - but it is a very real and potentially debilitating stage of life.

He is searching for something, but he doesn't know where to start.

What is the classic picture? In his 14th Century masterpiece, *The Divine Comedy*, Dante describes a man "halfway on the journey" of his life who is lost in dark woods. The lost man sees a light faraway that he senses is the answer for him, but he has to go on a psychological and spiritual journey in order to reach it. Assagioli, too, saw the crisis of meaning as a spiritual opportunity in his brilliant essay, *Self-Realization and Psychological Disturbances* (1965). Our comments draw on his words and our own clinical experience.

Before the crisis, the person has taken life as it comes and doesn't spend much time contemplating its meaning or purpose. He has focused on the satisfaction of his personal desires and ambitions. If he is reasonably socialized, he deflects some of his self-centered impulses in favor of the needs of others.

Possibly he thinks of himself as vaguely religious or spiritual. He more or less believes in God, but his religion is conventional. Once he has taken part in the scheduled rituals, he doesn't think much more about it.

His real belief is in the reality of the physical and social world which he participates in everyday. He is strongly attached to material things and considers material reality to be the only reality there is. His belief in a future "heaven" or afterlife is at best hypothetical but useful to imagine when fears of mortality rise up in him.

But then something begins to happen. He becomes both surprised and disturbed by a change in his emotional life. This may take place after a series of disappointments or from a shock such as the loss of a dear friend or important job. It can also be triggered by an illness in which he has to suspend his usual activities, or by a symbolic birthday (usually ages 50 or 60) in which the passing of time becomes very real to him. But, as in the case of Whitmore's business executive, it happens just as often without any apparent reason.

The change begins with a sense of restlessness, of dissatisfaction, of lack, but not the lack of anything material or specific. It is something vague and elusive that he is unable to describe. To this is added, by degrees, a growing boredom with everyday routines. Personal and professional interests, which formerly absorbed him, begin to lose their value.

The change begins with a sense of restlessness, of dissatisfaction, of lack, but not the lack of anything material or specific.

New questions come up that he would have never asked before:

- What is the point of living the way I do?
- Why should I keep on repeating my life the way it is now?

- Am I settling for a life that's too safe?
- Am I wasting my life?
- Is this it?
- What's the point?
- Isn't there more?

Sometimes, the questioning extends beyond his personal concerns:

- Why is there so much suffering?
- What's the reason for all the injustices in the world?
- Why is the world the way it is?

Quiet Panic

When the person has reached this point, he is apt to misunderstand his condition. Many who don't grasp the significance of these changes judge them as negative. The changes *are* negative in the way that he feels, but something positive is trying to get through to him. He doesn't yet get the message.

Alarmed at something unknown happening to him, he may make frantic efforts to re-attach himself to the "reality" of ordinary life that seems to be losing its point. Often he'll throw himself into seeking new challenges at work, aiming for greater levels of status, and getting involved with extreme experiences of physical or emotional novelty.

The caricature picture of the crisis – the middle-aged man buying a flashy car or working out obsessively in the gym in order to look young again - begin to show up at this point. These frantic efforts are reinforced by a consumerist culture which bombards us with products promising to help "turn back the clock" and make us feel younger and happier. The fact that the clock of our lifetime is ticking is part of the crisis, but trying to disguise it is exactly the wrong choice.

> The fact that the clock of our lifetime is ticking is part of the crisis, but trying to disguise it is exactly the wrong choice.

What is going on? The crisis is produced by the fact that the person has been living within society's version of reality and has suddenly uncovered the vulnerability and limited time of his actual life. This crisis, before revealing itself in its positive form of transpersonal wisdom, makes itself felt negatively. It shows how every self-centered goal, even a good goal, is transient. It shows that any wish about how you want life to be is illusory. The crisis is the dawning of maturity.

But our classic person in crisis resists this growing understanding. He does not want to give up on the things that make him feel good, even though realistically they are all changing and passing away in the natural flux of life.

At this point, it is not unusual for our person to consider a dramatic change in his life. He may want to divorce his wife, change his profession, move to another part of the country or have an entirely different lifestyle. (Fantasies of having a different life are common even without the midlife crisis.) In more difficult situations, he may start using drugs and/or alcohol excessively. In extreme cases, the idea of a painless terminal illness or even suicide as an escape from the trap of his current life comes to him seriously for the very first time.

People, of course, vary widely in how this crisis is manifested. There are many who never reach an acute stage, while others arrive at it almost overnight. There are also the simmering lifelong crisis. The person has always felt that there is more to life than surviving and functioning but doesn't know how to experience it.

For some, signs of their crisis are primarily mental - an unusual amount of doubts and indecision. In others, emotional indifference to what they used to care about is the most obvious feature. In some cases, the internal stress of the crisis produces physical symptoms, such as tension headaches, insomnia, agitation, anxiety, and/or digestive disturbances, and the first person they seek out for help is their medical doctor. The doctor will hopefully be successful in alleviating the physical symptoms, but the root cause will remain unexplored.

The Cure for the Crisis

The cure for the mid-life crisis is the discovery of life purpose. The person moves out of a disheartened state and feels a new energy for life. Even in the worst of times, connection to your life purpose helps you to rise above your circumstances: "What happens is never as important as what matters." (Grossman, 2012).

Since we started this discussion with Dante's man lost in the dark woods, here is how Dante describes the return of purpose (Schaub & Schaub, 2003):

> "As little flowers from the frosty night
> are closed and limp,
> and when the sun shines down on them,
> they rise to open on their stem,
> my wilted strength began to bloom within me,
> and such warm courage
> flowed into my heart
> that I spoke like a
> man set free."

The result is more than poetic. A recent research report, "Purpose in Life and Reduced Risk of Myocardial Infarction among Older U.S. Adults with Coronary Heart Disease: A Two-Year Follow-Up," indicates that having a feeling of purpose in life may help to protect against

My wilted strength began to bloom within me (Photo credits: George Schaub).

heart attacks among older American adults with coronary heart disease (Kim, et al., 2012). In the study, researchers surveyed more than 1,500 older adults with coronary heart disease and followed up after two years to investigate the association between purpose, which is typically conceptualized as a person's sense of direction and meaning in life, and the occurrence of a heart attack. The study found a significantly reduced risk of heart attack among participants who reported a higher sense of meaning.

The Difference between Meaning and Purpose

Meaning is important for motivating you, but it always turns out to be temporary.

You assign meaning to something of value, such as putting your children through college, but then they finish. You put energy and meaning into promotions at work, but then you get the promotion and it isn't what you thought it would be. You assign meaning to making more money so that you can retire sooner. One year later, you are approaching retirement - but retirement in order to do what, be what? Retirement without goals or structure suddenly looks boring. It was a goal without any deeper purpose to it.

Meaning is the key to keeping you focused, but it isn't deep enough in your nature to be truly satisfying. Satisfaction requires purpose.

Purpose

If you think of meaning as something you assign to life, purpose is something that life assigns to you. Meaning is produced by your socially-conditioned personality. Life purpose is a quality in your transpersonal nature.

Purpose is a sense of a calling, of something in you that quietly demands expression. It is the feeling of what you are supposed to become. Throw one little tomato seed onto concrete, and it will still spend the rest of its life trying to become a tomato. It is trying to do what it was born to do. That's you when you are in touch with your purpose. No matter what obstacles are put in your way, you keep trying to satisfy the potential that you feel inside you and that pushes at you to be expressed.

One young woman, interviewed on television about her preparations to climb a mountain, said that she was just trying to "become the *me* I'm supposed to be." Purpose doesn't have to be grand or even recognized by others. Perhaps the "me" the young woman climber seeks to be is a "me" who conquers her fears.

The further
away you
feel from
purpose, the
greater sense
of *something
missing. It's easy
to misinterpret*
this *missing*
feeling.

The further away you feel from purpose, the greater sense of *something missing*. It's easy to misinterpret this *missing* feeling. You can think it means there is a special place not yet travelled to, a site not yet seen, a food or sexual experience not yet had, a recognition not yet won, or a goal not yet reached.

Having worked for forty years as psychotherapists in Manhattan and its suburbs with hundreds of professional high achievers, we've seen many times that the search for what's missing must first exhaust itself outwardly. In a consumerist culture such as 21st Century America, the answer is assumed to be obtainable *out there*. One client reflected this exhausted search so well. Gazing at the new, large house he'd just had built for himself, he heard this thought so clearly in his mind: *Now what?*

This *sense of something missing* is the reason why Thoreau's quote is so often cited: "Most men lead lives of quiet desperation…" Less cited, but of equal importance, is the conclusion of his comment: "…and go to the grave with the song still in them."

No one wants Thoreau's diagnosis. It challenges you to look at your own life and to bring the awareness of your "song," your purpose, into full consciousness.

The Origin of Purpose

You are conditioned to think of yourself self-consciously. You are very aware of your height, weight, face and other physical features, and you are conscious that people make assumptions about you based on your appearance. You are conscious that your name and skin color reveal a social category or ethnic background, and you are vigilant about the opinions others have about your identity. In the privacy of your own mind, you have memorized beliefs about who you are because of what has been said to you in the past. The younger you were when the statements were made to you, the deeper the degree of their impression on you. Highly intelligent adults can walk around burdened by the belief that they are stupid because as a child they were told so enough times by an angry parent or teacher.

Societal myths also play a big part in your sense of self. In America, for example, the great myth of *being a success vs. being a failure* is reinforced repeatedly. People are *winners and losers*. By the age of 21, with their whole lives ahead of them, young people can get stuck already thinking of themselves as failures and losers, the American myth bearing down on them.

There are genetic, familial, social and mythic sources of self-consciousness and identity formation. They affect you, can even dominate you, and yet they are devoid of any lasting value. They aren't essential, and they aren't your real nature.

Evolution is one of the forces that moves inside creation and, in you, evolution is personally experienced as the drive toward purpose.

Your real nature is that you are a created being who is part of creation. This is your true identity. You have been, are, and always will be part of creation. It is why, when you walk in the woods or float in the ocean, you feel more like your basic self, at home in the world and at home in your own skin. You come from creation, live in it, and return to it. You participate in creation's cycle of birth, growth, decline, and death. You live inside its laws, its seasons, and its rhythms. This is who you really are, and it's all right.

Embedded in creation, you are moved by what moves inside creation. Evolution is one of the forces that moves inside creation and, in you, evolution is personally experienced as the drive toward purpose. Your desire for a purposeful life, a life that matters, is evolution moving you. It is beyond your wishes or ideas. It is what creation wants. In traditional language, you can say it is God's Will.

If you say *Yes* and respond to the inner drive toward purpose, you will experience the well-being of a life well-lived. Something truly real in you, your connection to creation, will be satisfied. Even in your time of dying, this deep soul satisfaction will be with you. You will know that you truly lived. The people around you will feel it, too.

If you ignore your life purpose, it doesn't mean it will leave you alone. It is a force in you, not an option. You will be stuck living with a dissatisfied, nagging feeling, no matter how busy you are, that you are missing out on something and that, with the passing of the years, you are failing to get to something that truly matters: "Most men lead lives of quiet desperation and go to the grave with the song still in them."

We need meaning in order to motivate ourselves to meet the demands of society. We need purpose in order to feel fulfillment in life.

Meaning, Purpose and the Transpersonal

Executive coach pioneer Whitmore observed that some of his clients, despite achieving their goals, were still dissatisfied and looking for something more. Whitmore determined that they had "hit the crisis wall" – the crisis of meaning and purpose.

To learn how to identify his clients' deeper purpose in life, Whitmore began to train in the pioneering transpersonal practices of Dr. Roberto Assagioli of Florence, Italy. The effectiveness of adding aspects of Assagioli's work to his coaching led Whitmore to conclude:

> "I am strongly recommending to the coaching establishment that the qualification criteria for all coaches include a section on the transpersonal" (Whitmore, 2009, p. 220).

Background on Roberto Assagioli (1888-1974)

In our search for new answers for our clients, we came upon Assagioli's work being taught in New England, just as Whitmore did in England. We learned how to apply Assagioli's transpersonal model to psychotherapy, our profession at the time, as Whitmore did to coaching. What most impressed us about Assagioli's commitment to the transpersonal was how much it helped him personally during a very low and dark period in his life. For us, he represents an embodiment of the gentle power of life purpose. It is in this spirit that we want to tell you more about him.

What most impressed us about Assagioli's commitment to the transpersonal was how much it helped him personally during a very low and dark period in his life.

Roberto Marco Grego Assagioli was born in the Jewish ghetto in Venice in 1888. He was two when his father died and a teenager when his mother died. He was adopted by his stepfather, a physician, and guided toward medical school at age 16. He went on to become a psychiatrist and student of psychoanalysis. His psychiatry residency supervisor was Carl Jung, and they went on to become lifelong colleagues. In 1909, Assagioli was named the Italian representative of the Vienna Psychoanalytic Society founded by Freud, the then controversial father of psychoanalysis.

Assagioli quickly became dissatisfied with psychoanalysis because, for him, it ignored the healthier possibilities inherent in human nature, including higher consciousness and spirituality. At the age of only twenty-two, he was already shaping his own vision of cultivating human development. He broke with the psychoanalytic movement and began to formulate his own practice of psychotherapy - psychosynthesis. Assagioli chose the term to indicate the synthesis of personality study and transpersonal study. Others viewing his work also feel that he created a synthesis between Eastern meditative practices and Western psychotherapeutic practices. He founded the first institute for teaching psychosynthesis in 1928 in Rome.

At the start of World War Two in Europe, he was falsely labeled a pacifist and jailed by the Fascists. He spent time in solitary confinement where he attained enlightenment

(Schaub & Schaub, 1994). In his notes from prison, he wrote:

"A sense of boundlessness, of no separation from all that is, a merging with the self of the whole. A sense of universal love. A wonderful merging. No separation - only differing aspects of wonder...

"Essential Reality is so far above all mental conceptions. It is inexpressible. It has to be lived. Joy inherent in Life Itself, in the very Substance of Reality...The realization of the Self, resting and standing in itself...The selfless Self...merged into God...the realization of our true self."

He came to regard his imprisonment as "a blessing":

"...the realization of independence from circumstances, the realization of inner freedom. We should realize the freedoms from fear, want, etc., but the right emphasis should be given that inner freedom without which all others are not sufficient. My dedication is going to be to the task of helping men and women to free themselves from inner prisons..."

Friends finally secured Assagioli's release, but his troubles were far from over. He remained under strict police scrutiny.

With the advent of the Nazi occupation, he was forced into hiding with his wife and only child, Ilario, in the mountains of northern Italy. His institute was dynamited, and many of his writings disappeared or were destroyed. With the arrival of the Allied Forces, Italy was liberated in August, 1944. In the last phase of the war, he directed a neurological hospital in Holland.

In 1946, he moved with his family to a house on Via San Domenico in Florence, which served as his home and the revitalized Institute of Psychosynthesis. A few years later, his son died from tuberculosis which he'd contracted while hiding in the mountains during the war.

Despite his many losses, Assagioli emerged as a man of deep peace and joy. He led many conferences, trained professionals, and conducted a worldwide correspondence (pre-email, of course), supporting meditation and psychology groups and writing books and articles on psychospiritual development.

Assagioli was the first modern Western doctor to incorporate worldwide spiritual and meditative practices directly into his work with patients. By the late 1950s, word of his approach had spread, and professionals began to seek him out as a teacher. His students in turn became teachers, and slowly institutes developed around the world.

At the end of Assagioli's life, he still called psychosynthesis a work in progress and left it to be expanded upon by the creativity of others. He insisted on not organizing it as a movement.

His long-time assistant, Luisa Lunelli, summarized his life this way:

"He was esteemed by so many, but few people knew him. He was a reserved gentleman, and essentially a solitary scholar. What we need to do now is to penetrate to the great secret of his life and find the way to this ocean of love that he brought to everyone he met."

Applications of Psychosynthesis

Since he was a psychiatrist, the most direct application of Assagioli's model is for psychotherapists, both for those who want to find a primary orientation and for those who want to enrich their current approach. Psychiatrists and psychologists in Italy became the early teachers of his work.

European physicians specializing in oncology were especially drawn to his concept of "sub-personalities," i.e., competing patterns in opposition to each other within the personality.

They speculated that such internal conflicts might be contributing to a weakened immune system, stomach disorders, and other stress-related issues, a concept since studied under the categories of psychosomatic medicine and mind-body medicine.

Another area Assagioli had written about was education. Some educators brought psychosynthesis into education of the gifted and the awakening of dormant possibilities in all students.

Some educators brought psychosynthesis into education of the gifted and the awakening of dormant possibilities in all students.

Clergy have incorporated his imagery and meditation practices to bring more direct spiritual experience to their congregants. Artists have utilized his imagery practices to enter deeper into the creative realm of the mind.

We adapted psychosynthesis for people in recovery from addictions and have taught the resulting model, *The Vulnerability Model of Recovery* (Schaub & Schaub, 1997), to treatment centers internationally. We have also used psychosynthesis as a theoretical framework, because of its integration of psychological and spiritual growth, in teaching the clinical uses of meditation and imagery.

The emergence of coaching as a new profession has added another use for Assagioli's model, with Whitmore as one example. Coaching is a very fitting use of psychosynthesis because Assagioli always intended his work to be psychoeducational. He wanted to take the basic principles of self-care and inner development and guide clients in using these principles for themselves. Within the field of coaching, integrative nurse coach training (Schaub, Luck & Dossey, 2012) emphasizes Assagioli's use of awareness practices to enhance both nurse coach self-care and mindful presence in their work with clients.

Practices

In the next section, we guide you through fourteen (14) **Huntington Method** practices. They are adapted from many meditative and spiritual sources and from Roberto Assagioli's pragmatic variations on meditative practices.

Assagioli assumed that most of his clients were not going to become disciplined practitioners of meditation. He therefore wanted to shape the practices so that clients would get at least a taste of the transpersonal discoveries waiting inside them. Like him, we have spent our careers in healthcare and mental health, and we have always stayed mindful of how to make the practices practical and easy to teach.

The practices we offer you have passed the test of safety and effectiveness in hospitals, clinics, schools, business wellness programs and private practice.

PART TWO:

The Huntington Method

Five Stage Process

Transpersonal development is the skill of guiding clients deeper into their nature. It is a five stage process:

1) establishing a state of inner peace which clears the way through the mind's usual activities;

2) learning to work with the mind's troubling thoughts in a new way;

3) gaining access to guiding inner wisdom;

4) realizing your life purpose and stabilizing it in your mind and feelings;

5) experiencing oneness and the energy of awareness itself.

This is a proven set of practices for making transpersonal discoveries:

Inner peace

Let Go

Body Scan

Centering

Working with the Mind

Stream of Consciousness

Centering and Naming

Defeating Difficult Thoughts

Pain Management

Inner Wisdom

Inner Wisdom

Time of Meaning

Mountain Path

Life Purpose

Hope/Deeper Hope

Intention Meditation

Oneness and the Energy of Awareness

Awareness Itself

Center of Awareness

Inner Peace

Inner peace is not a luxury. It is a daily necessity in order to maintain your integrity.

—*ROBERTO ASSAGIOLI*

Inner peace is relaxing, but it is far more than relaxation. As an experience, it is a state of dynamic stillness. You are aware, awake, and capable of noticing your internal experiences and external stimuli at subtler levels.

Inner peace brings quantifiable benefits to your mind, body and feelings. This is verified by over thirty years of meditation research. Stress, fear, and worry in the mind are relaxed. Stress-related physical symptoms – gastrointestinal distress, tight muscles, rapid heart rate – are reduced. Emotional struggles with doubt, uncertainty and nervousness are calmed down.

The benefits of inner peace are relevant across your lifespan. For the 14 year old, inner peace helps her to focus easier on a school test. For the shy twenty-five year old, inner peace allows him to participate more easily in social events. For the seriously ill 80 year old, inner peace gives him equanimity in facing the end of his life.

In transpersonal development, we cultivate inner peace for both 1) its calming effects, and 2) to create the conditions to gain access to your guiding inner wisdom.

The question naturally arises: if guiding wisdom is already in you, why don't you notice it more often? The answer is because of the mind's usual activities. The mind is ceaselessly processing stimuli from the outside world, from your body sensations, and from your own thoughts and imagination. All of this activity obscures access to guiding inner wisdom, which is a subtler level of the mind.

The question naturally arises: if guiding wisdom is already in you, why don't you notice it more often? The answer is because of the mind's usual activities.

Inner peace is necessary to quiet down the mind's usual activities, and your awareness itself is the way to inner peace.

AWARENESS IS THE SOURCE OF INNER PEACE

"Know the one thing that liberates everything – awareness itself." —DUDJOM RINPOCHE

It is normal to associate your mind with your thinking, but your mind has a deeper process – your awareness. Your awareness notices what you are thinking, but it doesn't think. It notices feelings in the body, but it isn't those feelings. Right now, as you read this, you are aware of yourself reading, but your awareness is not reading. Instead, your awareness is concurrently noticing what you are reading, noticing what you think of it, noticing how you feel about it, noticing the room you are in, and so on. Awareness notices what is going on, but it isn't any of those things that are going on.

You can't see your awareness. You can't touch it, you can't feel it. To date, researchers have not been able to find it in the brain. Awareness remains a physiological mystery. Yet it is not a mystery in our daily experience. Quite the contrary: it is always with you, always working for you, always noticing. And if you didn't have awareness, you would have no experience at all. You only have experience because you have awareness. Awareness is the basis of experience. Despite its primal reality, awareness isn't something that you can see or get our hands on, and yet it makes everything exist for you.

You rarely get to experience awareness itself. It is usually occupied by paying attention to your various mental and physical activities. When you use a practice that cultivates inner peace, however, your usual mind and body activities quiet down. In such moments, awareness is temporarily freed up, and you get to experience the special quality of awareness itself.

Awareness itself is naturally serene. This discovery is the reason that all of the meditative traditions, East and West, emphasize awareness practices and seek to enter a state of awareness itself (Bauer, 2011). These practices are variously called contemplation, concentration, presence, mindfulness, silence, one-pointedness, liberation.

When you enter a state of awareness itself, all mind and body stimuli fall away. All you are aware of is being aware. You're not asleep, you're not in a trance, you are wide awake. You are aware of awareness. If deepened, awareness of awareness is considered to be the road to enlightenment. Personally knowledgeable about the importance of this discovery, Assagioli developed several practices to introduce clients to awareness of awareness.

Modern medical and psychological research brings an addition to the traditional knowledge about awareness. Placing awareness practices under the general term *mindfulness*, the research emphasizes the practical uses of awareness to reduce people's suffering (see, for example, Greeson, 2008). If a student can't focus on tests at school or an adult can't concentrate at work, awareness practices can help. If people suffer from negative narratives in their mind that create obstacles to moving forward in life, awareness practices can help to free them from the grip of these self-defeating narratives (Farb et al., 2008). If a person suffers from poor memory, awareness practices can improve it (Jha et al., 2010).

All of the practices in this section, **Inner Peace**, are based on the client's cultivation of being relaxed and aware.

PRACTICE 1: LET GO

Let Go is an introductory practice to help clients to calm down their mind and body. It gets a good response because of its simplicity and the ability to do it anywhere at any time.

Steps

1. Close your eyes or at least lower your eyes…

2. Now give way to the chair…Let the chair hold you…

3. Now let your shoulders drop…

4. Now I am going to ask you to say a three-word phrase over and over again in your mind…

5. The first word is your first name, and the next two words are "let go"…Your first name, followed by "let go"…

6. You can link the three-word phrase to your in-breath, or out-breath, or not link it to your breath at all. Find the way you like best…

7. Your first name, followed by "let go"…repeating it over and over again in your mind…take your time…

Wait two minutes and then say, "And now let go of the practice and turn your attention toward noticing how you are…"

Wait thirty seconds and then say, "And when you feel ready, at your own pace, begin to come back to the room and open your eyes…"

Discussion. In our transpersonal work in Manhattan, we taught the **Let Go** practice to many clients in the aftermath of 9/11. Clients reported that it was a quick and effective technique as they approached the subway or an elevator or other situations which, post 9/11, had become triggers for fear and anxiety.

The repetition of this three word phrase involves no belief system or sect, but its origins are mantra meditation which is used in both Eastern and Western spiritual traditions. Mantra meditation is the repetition of a sacred phrase said aloud or silently in the mind. Often associated with yogic and Buddhist practices, it is also found in Eastern Orthodox, Roman Catholic and other traditions. In Roman Catholicism, for example, it is the repetition of prayers linked to the beads of a rosary.

One form of mantra meditation, transcendental meditation (TM), was the focus of cardiologist Benson's early research at Harvard (1975). Finding that the TM mantra meditation evoked a relaxation response, Benson went on to modify the Sanskrit words of the mantra. He then experimented with simple, positive statements devoid of any spiritual implications. He demonstrated in his research that a relaxation response could be evoked by any combination of simple, positive statements said repetitively in the mind.

There is controversy around such an approach in which a practice is reduced and stripped of its spiritual tradition. Since all of the mind-body meditation practices have their origins in spiritual traditions (Schaub, 1995), it means that every practice you study in this book will have a similar history of reductionism.

There is a pragmatic reason for this. Secular health and wellness professionals who want to offer these beneficial practices work in a multi-cultural society. While you as the professional may be open to various spiritual traditions, it does not follow that clients will feel the same way. You must therefore present only the essential aspects of a practice without reference to its spiritual background. The spiritual tradition itself may not mean anything to a particular client and may even interfere with the client's acceptance of the practice.

This reductionism does not imply disrespect for the spiritual traditions themselves. Quite the contrary: the secularization of a spiritual practice is an acknowledgment of its value and a desire to offer it to the widest variety of clients who need help.

PRACTICE 2: BODY SCAN

This practice brings several benefits: it is calming and focusing; it helps you to connect with your awareness as you move it throughout your body; you learn how you can have control of your awareness.

Steps

1. Begin by putting your feet on the floor and making your back fairly straight but not stiff...now lower or close your eyes...

2. Now bring your awareness to your feet...

3. Now bring awareness to your left leg from your left foot all the way up to your left hip...

4. Now bring awareness to your right leg from your right foot all the way up to your hip...

5. Now bring awareness to your genitals and pelvic area...

6. Now bring to awareness to the sensations of your stomach...

7. And now to your chest and your shoulders...

8. And now let awareness extend from your left shoulder down your left arm to your hand...

9. And now let awareness extend from your right shoulder down your right arm to your hand...awareness of arms and hands...

10. And now begin to bring awareness to your neck and throat...

11. And now to the sensations of your face...

12. And now your mouth...

13. And now your nostrils and your breath...awareness of breath...

14. And now to your left eye...

15. And now moving awareness to your right eye...

16. And now bring awareness to the space between your eyebrows…

17. And now to the middle of your forehead…sensations at the middle of your forehead…

18. And now bring awareness to the top of your head, noticing the sensations up there…

19. And now, at your own pace, slowly begin to guide awareness downward from the top of your head, guiding it slowly, gently, distributing it throughout your face… and slowly, gently, throughout your entire self…take your time…

Wait two minutes and then say, "Now begin to notice how you are right now…

Wait one minute and then say, "When you feel ready, begin to open your eyes..."

Discussion. This is a lengthy practice. You can shorten it by focusing on only a few aspects of the body.

The overall purpose of the **Body Scan** is to connect you to awareness itself. As stated earlier, awareness itself is serene, and so the **Body Scan** puts you in touch with a serene part of your nature.

Clients will sometimes have energy experiences while doing the **Body Scan**. They will feel sensations and energy releases or movement and feel refreshed afterwards. In this way, the **Body Scan** is a kind of mental acupuncture, moving energy in your body. These energy experiences in turn point you toward another of your transpersonal resources – *experiencing oneness*. This will be discussed more fully in the **Oneness** section of the **Huntington Method.**

PRACTICE 3: CENTERING

Adapted from QiGong, this practice introduces a deeper state of relaxation. As you will see, this leads to the gradual freedom from pre-occupying thoughts and feelings.

Steps

1. Gently shake your hands for a while…

2. Now place one hand just under your navel and place your other hand on top of the first hand…

3. Now slowly let your awareness go down to your hands and notice the sensations of one hand touching the other…

4. Now begin to notice the rising and falling of your belly underneath your hands…Let yourself become interested in the sensations of the rising and falling…Nothing else to do…Nothing special has to happen…Just noticing the rising and falling…

Wait three minutes and then say, "And now let go of the practice and turn your attention to noticing how you are…"

Wait thirty seconds and then say, "And when you feel ready, at your own pace, begin to come back to the room…"

Discussion. In a recent experience of teaching clinical meditation at a Veterans Administration hospital, this "hands on belly" proved to be the favorite practice. A television news report featured the training, and the veteran selected to demonstrate meditation for the cameras also chose the hands on belly practice for its effectiveness and simplicity.

Working with the Mind

Despite the fact that you live with it your entire life, no one educates you about your mind. All day and all night, your mind produces thoughts, ideas, images, urges, associations, imaginings, and it is an ongoing question of what to pay attention to. School and work settings emphasize the use of your mind to memorize and think rationally, skills which help you to fit into society. Beyond these skills, however, your mind holds the transpersonal qualities of inner peace, inner wisdom, life purpose, and oneness.

These next practices create the basic conditions for discovering these health-giving qualities.

PRACTICE 4:
STREAM OF CONSCIOUSNESS

Stream of Consciousness is first done by you, the professional, in front of the client. By doing so, your client sees the simplicity and low demand of the practice. Your willingness to practice in front of your client also communicates a spirit of collaboration on this journey into transpersonal experiences.

Steps

(You do this first)

1. Make yourself comfortable in your chair and close your eyes...

2. Now begin to say out loud whatever comes into your awareness...Don't need to explain it...just name it... (E.g., I notice an itch...I notice daydreaming...)

After you have demonstrated it for two minutes, elicit any questions, and then ask the client to try it. Let the client do this for two minutes and then ask the client to stop and open his or her eyes.

Discussion. As simple as the practice may appear, you are actually introducing a profound teaching to your clients. The act of noticing that something comes into awareness, to then be replaced by the next thing that comes into awareness, to then be replaced by the next thing, etc., demonstrates the flux of the mind, feelings and sensations. Through demonstrating this state of flux to your client, you are introducing an inner resource – the ceaseless presence of awareness itself - that is deeper than the passing thoughts and sensations. Thoughts, feelings, urges, and sensations all come and go, come and go, and yet your awareness it always there, always present. You can tell a client this, and they may intellectually understand it, but the goal here is to have the client directly experience it.

The **Stream of Consciousness** is then expanded by doing the same noticing and naming practice, except this time they will not say anything out loud and will only verbalize it in the privacy of their minds.

Steps

1. Make yourself comfortable in your chair and close your eyes…

2. Now begin to notice whatever comes into your awareness and name it in the privacy of your mind…Just notice it and name it and then wait to see what comes next…If nothing comes, that's fine…Nothing special to do here…Nothing has to happen…Just noticing and naming…

Wait two minutes and then ask your client to stop and to open his or her eyes.

Discussion. With **Stream of Consciousness**, you have introduced clients to the concept that they can notice and name their thoughts and sensations without getting involved with them.

In our experience, clients initially find this practice to be a curiosity. So accustomed to following their thoughts and feelings, it is a new mental action to notice them and let them go. It isn't the same as trying to ignore thoughts. It is deciding not to give them attention and energy.

The **Stream of Consciousness** practice is quietly powerful for clients who are troubled by their thoughts. Treating thoughts as insubstantial passing events rather than as reflections of who you are, clients gain more control over their mental life.

You cannot prevent thoughts from showing up, but you can invite them to leave. Once clients grasp this possibility, their inner peace deepens. It is liberating to realize that you have more choice than you thought you had.

PRACTICE 5:
CENTERING AND NAMING

This builds on **Practices 2, 3** and **4**.

Centering and Naming is a variation on mindfulness. Defined by Jon Kabat-Zinn, a pioneer of bringing meditation into healthcare, mindfulness is "the practice of paying attention, on purpose, in the present moment, without judgment" (1991).

Mindfulness practices typically use the breath in the nostrils as a way to focus your attention. When a thought or sensation pulls you away from the breath in your nostrils, you notice and name the thought or sensation, and then return your attention to the breath in your nostrils. You are still using the **Stream of Consciousness** practices of noticing and naming, but now you have added a centering practice - the focus on breath.

We prefer to focus on the rising and falling of the belly, as we did in **Practice 3: Centering**, rather than focus on the nostrils. Our experience is that attention focused on the rising and falling of the belly has two advantages:

- It provides a deeper degree of relaxation;
- When you focus on the breath in your nostrils, it is easy to slip seamlessly into your mind and drift off into thought. It is much more obvious when thoughts have pulled your attention away from your belly.

Steps

1. Gently shake your hands for a while…
2. Now place one hand just under your navel and place your other hand on top of the first hand…

3. Now slowly let your awareness go down to your hands and notice the sensations of one hand touching the other...

4. Now begin to notice the rising and falling of your belly underneath your hands...

5. Let yourself become interested in the sensations of the rising and falling...Nothing else to do...Nothing special has to happen...Just noticing the rising and falling...

6. If a thought or sensation or distraction pulls you away from your belly, name the thought or sensation or distraction and then return to noticing the rising and falling...

Wait three minutes and then say, "And now let go of the practice and turn your attention to noticing how you are..."

Wait thirty seconds and then say, "And when you feel ready, at your own pace, begin to come back to the room..."

Discussion. When you engage with a thought, you energize it. Assagioli called this *identifying* with the thought. When you treat the thought by noticing it, naming it, and then leaving it to return to your breath, you de-energize the thought, which Assagioli called *disidentification* (Assagioli, 1965). You are not trying to ignore or deny your thoughts. You are noticing them, but then you are choosing not to stay with them. You are not giving them your mind's energy.

Centering and Naming is a deceptively simple practice with liberating implications. For example, if a client is in recovery from alcoholism, he or she must learn how to deal in a new way with thoughts of drinking. If the client identifies with and engages with the drinking thought, it will inspire images and urges to act on the thought (Assagioli, 1974). Instead, if the client notices it and names it as a drinking thought and then returns his or her awareness to the breath, the drinking thought will be deprived of the mind's energy.

Of course, the drinking thinking doesn't just go away. It was an obsessive thought that was linked for years to the compulsive use of alcohol. But now the client has a tool: each time the drinking thought rises in the mind, the **Centering and Naming** practice de-energizes it. The old habit of identifying with the thought turns into a new habit of disidentifying from the thought. This same principle applies to all harmful thoughts.

PRACTICE 6: DEFEATING DIFFICULT THOUGHTS

Defeating Difficult Thoughts is a psychoeducational aspect of the **Huntington Method**. You use **Centering and Naming** for the actual practice, but you add knowledge of fear, stress and anxiety in your instructions to the client. By offering this knowledge, the client can more clearly notice when fear-based thoughts, feelings, or sensations are rising up in them and can more easily name them.

Psychoeducation on Difficult Thoughts

The following information summarizes the essential features of fear, stress and anxiety. You can choose from it what is most pertinent for a particular client. You can educate your clients about the causes and manifestations of fear, and you can help them to recognize the patterns in their mind and body which reveal that fear is dominating them.

We start with the neuroscience of fear.

Brain research. Brain research is giving us an enlightening map of the interaction between fear and the way your brain/mind/body reacts to it.

Fear is natural and normal. It is an alarm system hard-wired in your brain. This alarm system is part of your survival instinct, and it is referred to in brain research as the brain's *fear circuitry*. This fear circuitry is observable through brain imaging (Shin & Liberzon, 2010).

The evolutionary reason for the existence of your fear circuitry is physical threat. The circuitry evolved as a brain function in order to scan for any signs of dangerous predators present in the environment. When an antelope smells the presence of a lion in the bush and reacts with alarm, it is the same signal that you experience when you notice some dangerous person hiding in the shadows of the street.

Threats don't only come from your outer environment. As you know from your personal experience, your own thoughts can scare you, which in turn activate your fear circuitry to send signals of alarm – worry, warnings and anxiety – into your mind and body.

Your fear circuitry can perceive/imagine threat in the most ordinary and momentary details such as a "look" someone gives you or a passing leg sensation. As a result, you often end up with anxiety about something that wasn't a threat at all.

These overestimates of threat happen because your fear circuitry does not think rationally: it only thinks fearfully. Your fear circuitry is an instinctive, survival-based brain function. It is vitally important to us but limited by its obsessive focus on threat.

The anxiety loop. The fear circuitry's vigilant scanning for threat causes you trouble when it generates *too much anxiety too often* and begins to interfere with your life.

Anxiety is a sudden and complex bio-chemical shift inside you which alerts you that something bad is about to happen to you. If you review your past experiences of anxiety, however, you will see that 99.9 % of the time, the *something bad* that actually happened to you was the awful feeling of the anxiety itself.

Nevertheless, the sudden shift into anxiety is disturbing. It often includes a racing heart, a light-headed and dazed mental state, weak knees and rubbery legs, a panicky trapped feeling, and a sense of impending doom. You temporarily lose your ability to think clearly and are thrown into an instinctual reaction of fight, flight or freeze.

Too many experiences of anxiety erode your confidence and create an anticipation that you will experience the anxiety again. In this way, anxiety breeds more anxiety. It insinuates itself into your life.

Once you have become *anxious about becoming anxious*, you are stuck in an anxiety loop. Your fear circuitry, vigilantly scanning for threat, has now added the feeling of anxiety itself as another threat.

The OCD anxiety loop. Within the general group of anxious clients, there are some whose sensitive nervous systems, imagination, and fear circuitry combine in a way that generates catastrophic fears into their minds and bodies on a frequent basis. The minds of these sensitive clients are like mirrors for the worst fears of the human race. Their fear circuitry can routinely produce intrusive and bizarre warnings about fatal illness, financial ruin, societal collapse, going insane, killing someone, killing themselves.

Clients intellectually understand that these warnings are extreme but still can't stop their production. Looking up a tall building, the client imagines what it would be like to jump off the top. Looking at water in a toilet bowl, the client has a flashing image of drinking the water. Other images flash by: choking their child; driving their car into the oncoming traffic; laying in their deathbed in a hospital. They are naturally disturbed that their mind produces such thoughts, and they are left to struggle with the high anxiety that such thoughts physiologically generate.

In reaction to such anxieties, these clients sometimes develop rituals. They get brief relief from such ritualistic acts as repeated handwashing, flicking a light switch ten times, or making sure all the papers on their desk are parallel to each other. They completely understand that the ritual has no real power to control reality but still feel compelled to perform it.

These sensitive clients are in an anxiety loop that is referred to as an obsessive-compulsive disorder (OCD). The OCD anxiety loop looks like this:

- frightening and sometimes bizarre thoughts
- the alarm and anxiety caused by such thoughts
- the compelling need to get rid of the anxiety
- rituals to get rid of the anxiety
- temporary relief
- the return of frightening and sometimes bizarre thoughts

Post-traumatic stress disorder. The Anxiety Loop and the OCD Anxiety Loop are considered to be caused by overactive fear circuitry: in other words, an internally-driven, intra-brain event. In contrast, Posttraumatic Stress Disorder (PTSD) is anxiety caused by disturbing outer events which have left the client susceptible to being *triggered* by reminders of those events. The *triggers* can be memories and sensations and/or outer situations that in any way resemble the original traumatizing events.

Unfortunately, events of traumatic proportions happen to more people than we may want to admit. Our daily news is filled with reports of violence in war and terrorist attacks, sadistic criminal acts, childhood physical and/or sexual abuse, natural disasters. The increased awareness of our veterans returning from war with PTSD has opened up a great interest in the best treatments and path of healing.

Factors adding to fear, stress and anxiety. The Anxiety Loop, the OCD Anxiety Loop, and the Post-Traumatic Stress Disorder are clear-cut issues that will motivate clients to ask for your help. As you assess their problems, you will want to note other factors that may be adding to their fear, stress and anxiety issues.

These factors can include:

- Emotional vulnerability
- The role of the imagination
- The genetic role of family history
- The role of natural sensitivity
- The role of superstitions
- The role of drugs
- The role of stimulants in the diet
- The underlying awareness of loss and suffering in life
- The underlying awareness of mortality

Emotional vulnerability. If you go into reactions of fight/flight/freeze even though no real danger is present, it doesn't mean your perception is totally inaccurate. For human beings, and for other higher intelligence animals as well, you can feel emotionally vulnerable to the degree to which you *imagine* your very survival is threatened. If the boss appears to be angry at you, it is far more than an unpleasant feeling. His anger may be a threat to your job and therefore your livelihood.

Work and financial insecurity are the major sources of emotional vulnerability and fight/flight/freeze in most people's day-to-day lives.

Emotional perceptions of threat and vulnerability are very individual. For Joe, the anticipation of taking a test triggers a profound alarm in him because it touches upon a deep-seated belief that he is stupid. Jane does not harbor such a negative belief about her intelligence, and so the anticipation of the test does not produce as much anxiety. Consequently, with less anxiety, Jane will probably do better on the test than the highly anxious Joe who fears that his test score will reveal that he is stupid.

It is a vicious cycle. Joe's belief that he is stupid leads to test-taking anxiety which leads to poorer performance which leads to further "proof" that he is stupid. Guided by this belief, he starts to avoid any situation which involves taking tests, he stays silent during a lively discussion, he hopes that no one notices him at a social gathering, and so on. By escaping/avoiding situations which might reveal him to be stupid, he minimizes experiences of anxiety but ends up reinforcing the fears about his intelligence. These fears become stabilized as a "truth" in his self-image.

The role of the imagination. As you know from your dreams, imagined scenes of fear are numberless. Gathering humanity's bad dreams together, you would have a film library of scenes of being chased, abandoned, lost, trapped, tortured, falsely accused, and humiliated, to varying degrees, on a nightly basis. Such imagined scenes in your dreams produce the same anxiety as if you were actually being threatened. If bad enough, they wake you up in the middle of the night. There you are, awakened by a bad dream, confused for a moment about which reality you are in, and then realizing you are alone in a dark room with the same mind that just a few minutes ago was scaring you to death with its imagined scenes.

There is a huge club, a world membership, of people awake and anxious at 3 a.m. If you are one of them, take some small comfort in realizing that you are not alone. We guarantee that there are millions of people awake with you.

There is a huge club, a world membership, of people awake and anxious at 3 a.m. If you are one of them, take some small comfort in realizing that you are not alone. We guarantee that there are millions of people awake with you.

The positive power of the imagination is also indisputable. It is the source of humanity's greatest achievements in art and science and the key to solving countless practical problems.

As only one brief example of the positive power of the imagination, medical research has proven for many years that imagining that a medicine will help you (even though you are being given a useless sugar pill) can be as effective as the actual medicine recommended for your medical condition. Known as the *placebo effect*, this "imagined" power of the useless sugar pill turns into a physical reality: the patient reports less compulsion to drink alcohol or less discomfort in their stomach because they believe in the pill.

The role of natural sensitivity. Sensitive clients have a lot going on inside them *at all times*. They tend to feel more, sense more, think more. They also tend to have their minds go to the dark places where most other people don't care to go – to the difficult facts of suffering, loss, and death that are everyone's destiny. They live a life in which they are negotiating just as much with their inner world as they are with the outer world.

Clients who are sensitive don't speak about their inner world because some of their fear-based thoughts and feelings, if revealed, may subject them to social embarrassment. Additionally, their inner joys may feel too intimate to admit to others. They are awed by both the beauty of the world and its incomprehensible cruelty.

Sensitive clients can appear to adapt well to daily life but deep down are always longing for something more, some answer to what they sense and feel. They may present themselves in a doctor's office with stomach pains or a therapist's office with an unhappy relationship, but underneath they are not looking for a doctor or a therapist but a guide to a way of being in harmony with the uncertainty built into life.

They often feel alone in their longing, but in fact there are more people like them than they realize. Sadly, they won't discover this because of their own reluctance to speak about their private inner world.

The role of superstitions. Many clients are unaware of the fact that in their ethnic or religious backgrounds there are stories, myths and beliefs about an evil force in the world. For example, clients from Mediterranean backgrounds have often been exposed to versions of the "evil eye," a force of evil that you ward off by having protective objects and images around the house (Dossey, 2009). Fundamentalist religious groups speak of the devil's presence in the world. Dictatorial leaders will invent superstitions and demonize a group within the population as a scapegoat for the problems of the region or country.

All such superstitions are driven by vulnerability and fear. It is worth exploring if the client remembers being exposed to such frightening views of life and other people.

The role of drugs. Drugs – whether legally prescribed, over-the-counter, or illegally bought on the street – can cause your body to have the same symptoms as anxiety. If your heart is racing, how can your fear circuitry possibly discern if it is perceiving a real threat or experiencing the effect of a non-drowsy cold formula? Multiple medications may cause disturbances in the gut and other symptoms which mimic the sensations of anxiety.

The role of stimulants in your diet. Caffeine, sugar, sweeteners and other common ingredients speed up your body's systems, making you feel jumpy and wired, a sensation associated with being anxious.

There is an exquisite interaction between your gut and your brain. Foods that disturb your stomach, perhaps in the form of allergic reactions to them, can lead to a feeling of brain fog, which is also a common symptom of anxiety. Your fear circuitry cannot discern the difference between a threat and a reaction to gluten. All it knows is that it is perceiving anxiety-like sensations in your body which in turn aggravates the *anxious-about-becoming-anxious* loop.

The underlying awareness of loss and suffering in life. Everyone lives with a feeling of vulnerability. All around you, you see proof that lives can be negatively changed in an instant by an accident, an illness, a big disappointment. No one wants to suffer or experience loss, and everyone will. As we described earlier in the role of natural sensitivity, some clients are more sensitive to these fears, which makes them more prone to significant degrees of anxiety. Entire philosophies and spiritual practices are based on trying to come to terms with these realities.

The underlying awareness of mortality. The world's religions all offer some image of an afterlife in order to soothe the universal fear of death. The finality of death and your personal annihilation are bewildering facts for your mind to grasp. We've heard many clients say *I'm not afraid of dying*, but when they are asked to imagine their personal annihilation, that is a disturbing and incomprehensible matter.

Even such a great thinker as Freud, when he deliberately challenged his mind to imagine his own nothingness, couldn't do it. The thought overwhelmed him. He concluded that either the mind can't imagine nothingness or, conversely, that there is no such thing as nothingness.

Loss, suffering and mortality are the basis of our fears and vulnerability in this world. No one is exempt from this vulnerability, but we all process its effect on us in different ways.

Some people react to vulnerability by becoming aggressive. They attempt to power over their vulnerability, a choice that we call being willful. Others react by trying to withdraw, escape, which we call being will-less. The third reaction, which we consider to be the balanced way, is being willing. Willingness is the act of facing the truth of our shared human vulnerability with peace and wisdom. We will return to this study of vulnerability when we outline the path of the **Huntington Method** in **Part Five**.

In this review of factors that add to fear, stress and anxiety, only two – drug use and stimulants in your diet – can be changed by new behaviors. All the others - vulnerability, imagination, genetics, natural sensitivity, superstitions, loss and suffering, mortality - require that you awaken your transpersonal resources to counteract these factors and help you to live with greater harmony.

Case Example: Joseph

Joseph, a young college student with self-described low self-esteem, wanted help to overcome his shyness and social struggles.

He was trained in **Centering and Naming**. He learned to notice and name the thoughts that actually comprised his low self-esteem. The thoughts involved 1) self-criticisms about his shyness, 2) worries that he wasn't accomplishing things in life (dating, career direction) as fast as others, and 3) beliefs that things won't work out for him because he is from "a loser family."

Before his training, Joseph would spend time ruminating on these difficult thoughts whenever they rose up in his mind. In Assagioli's terms, he was identifying with the thoughts as part of who he was.

With training, he learned to deprive them of energy. He came to name the harmful thoughts not as truths but as *sad stories* that his mind had made up in response to feeling anxious. As he sat in **Centering and Naming** practice, the old thoughts would rise, be labeled as sad stories, and he'd then return to the rising and falling of his breath. He'd learned how to disdentify from them.

You can see the possibility in this practice for a quiet revolution in the mind. The quiet revolution happens in the moment you realize that *the thought I am having right now is one I can identify with and give energy to – or choose not to. If I do not identify with the thought as me or mine, it loses energy and fades away.*

Changing difficult thoughts to neutral or rational thoughts is the essence of the cognitive-behavioral therapies. By recognizing negative and irrational thoughts and replacing them with new thoughts, you can change the way you feel.

The implications of **Centering and Naming** go further. If you are freeing your mind's energy from difficult thoughts, what happens to that energy? Your awareness in the present moment becomes stronger and more available to you. You feel more *here*, more connected to your immediate experience, more attentive to what is happening right now. In other words, you feel happier.

As of this writing, mindfulness-based practices are being researched and applied to physiologically changing the brain itself (Hoelzel et al., 2011). The results so far have been extremely encouraging. Through brain imaging, it has been established that eight weeks of mindfulness-based practice literally, physiologically, builds new integrative fibers in the executive center of your brain. The executive center is responsible for managing the reactivity of your fear circuitry. If the executive center is strengthened, it can manage your fear and reduce your stressors easier.

PRACTICE 7: PAIN MANAGEMENT

This practice utilizes the awareness you cultivate in **Centering and Naming** and applies it to reducing pain. In the case referred to in the following steps, a client was suffering from chronic neck and shoulder pain as the result of a job accident six months before.

Steps

1. Let's begin by allowing the chair to hold you…give way to the chair…

2. Now bring awareness to the middle of your chest…notice the sensations there…

3. Now guide awareness to the sensations of your face, noticing the sensations…And now to your mouth…sensations of your mouth…and now to your nostrils and the sensations of your breath…

5. Don't do anything to your breath…just let it be the way it is…

6. And now, under your control, gently guide your awareness from your breath to the pain in your shoulder… be willing to find the area with the most sensation… when you find it, place your awareness right into the core of the sensation and follow what happens… **(Client reports that the pain has moved to his upper arm.)**

7. Okay…now for a moment, guide your awareness back to your nostrils…and now guide your awareness right into the middle of the sensation and follow what happens…

The client reports that he can't find the pain. As he is talking, he again feels the pain in his shoulder. The practice is repeated and, again, the pain seems to be temporarily dissolved. He is baffled by what this means.

Discussion. There are two healing factors involved in this practice. The first is that the client is being empowered to work with the pain rather than being intimidated by it.

The second factor is that awareness is energy. We talked earlier about how your awareness can energize thoughts and how you can withdraw awareness-energy from difficult thoughts. When you direct awareness into a pain sensation, you are directing energy into that sensation and altering it. It may not make the pain go away, but it will alter the sensation in a palpable way. The client will feel a significant change.

These four practices for **Working with the Mind – Stream of Consciousness, Centering and Naming, Defeating Difficult Thoughts, Pain Management** – give you skills for clearing the way through your mind's usual activities. By doing so, you are creating the conditions for easier access to a subtler level of your mind – your guiding inner wisdom.

Inner Wisdom

"We are all crossing the vast ocean of being, each of us endowed with an inner knowing as our guide."

—*DANTE*

We've said earlier that the concept of inner wisdom requires some education. Who has ever taught you that you have an inner source of wise guidance, and that this guidance is directing you toward well-being and the purpose of your life? Because we aren't educated about it, guiding inner wisdom may sound like something in a fairy tale - a magical wizard or wisdom figure in long robes and white beard. It is in fact a process of mind that includes but goes beyond the rational. It is always available to you and always ready to direct you toward life-affirming choices and away from self-defeating patterns. The key is to know how to access it.

Discovering your inner wisdom is a leap of self-knowledge, a new development that is inspiring and encouraging. It means that something in you is participating in a process of evolving. It also means that, no matter how crazy and random the world may seem at times, you can always orient around your life purpose and go forward in life.

As early as the 1930s, Assagioli called for a science of the *higher self*, his term at that time for inner wisdom. Starting in 1978, we began to test out his inner wisdom ideas with clients. Gradually, we gathered many anecdotes from our work that pointed to three themes in inner wisdom experiences:

- Your inner wisdom's time orientation is to the future. The past only matters as lessons to contribute to the future.
- Your inner wisdom comes to you through words, images and/or energies (including emotions and physical sensations), with each person having their own individual style.
- The purpose of the wisdom is to guide you toward your life purpose.

Historical Context for Inner Wisdom Work

There is nothing new in the concept of guiding inner wisdom. It is the mystic's vision, the artist's muse, the scientist's intuition. The Old Testament prophets received it by seeing visions and hearing voices. Elijah referred to it as "the still small voice within." When Moses ascended the mountain to receive wisdom about how to lead his people and asked for a name to call the source of his guidance, he was told only, "Tell them that 'I Am' sent you."

Tibetan Buddhists call this internal wisdom *prajna*. The Zen tradition refers to the "inner reason of the universe which exists in each mind."

Gandhi meditated in order to receive guidance from what he called "the inner light" of universal truth. The *Kabbalah* of the Jewish mystics call this higher center of wisdom the *Tiferet*. Greek mythology speaks of it as the oracle. Dante, in *The Divine Comedy*, his masterful poetic description of spiritual realization, personified inner wisdom as his female guide, Beatrice.

In the 12 Steps of Alcoholics Anonymous, it is the "Higher Power." Carl Jung referred to it as "the Self," and, as we said, Assagioli initially called it the "higher self."

The practices developed to gain access to inner wisdom also have a cross-cultural dimension. People around the world have used varieties of dance, ceremonies, drugs, trance induction, dreaming, physical training, meditation, prayer, isolation, sensory deprivation, art, music, literature and many other means to open themselves to this higher or deeper level of the mind.

This myriad of practices confirms that guiding inner wisdom has been universally recognized as desirable and attainable. As you begin to explore your own inner wisdom, you can do so with the confidence that you are joining a timeless, worldwide lineage of students who have wanted to know more about this important human resource.

Case Example: Nancy

Perhaps you will recognize some aspects of yourself in Nancy, a client who was able to move from suffering to living with more courage and hope.

A high-level financial executive in her late forties and the mother of a son in college, Nancy was in a daily struggle with anxiety. She would feel it rising up inside her for no apparent reason at almost any time - a terrible sense of dread and impending doom. It might come while she was working quietly at her desk, waiting on line to see a movie, or just lying down to go to sleep. Because she didn't know when or why it might occur, she felt at its mercy, as if it was in charge of her life.

She'd already been to several medical doctors. They had ruled out early menopause or thyroid problems as possible reasons for her anxiety but had not yet found any other physical cause. She'd been prescribed a variety of medications, each of which seemed to work for two or three weeks, but sooner or later the anxiety would reassert itself. All she wanted, she said, was to feel "normal" again, to have her old self returned to her. Nothing she'd tried so far had been able to give her that.

At her first meeting with Richard, as Nancy was describing her anxiety, she suddenly began to feel it again in the middle of her chest. She said she hated the feeling. It depressed her to think that her life was being taken away by something that was beyond her control.

Richard asked her to close her eyes and to focus on the sensation. Then, after a few moments, she was asked to convert the sensation into a picture in her imagination. What would her anxiety look like?

She immediately saw a picture of a broken heart, a heart split in two. She was asked to find out from the broken heart what it needed to heal, and to be open to whatever response she saw or heard in her mind or felt in her body. Nancy reported that she saw children, flowers, sunshine, and then she said, "Innocence."

Asked to consider what *innocence* meant to her, she responded that she'd lost all innocence about life, that she now saw life as brutal, and that her heart was broken for three reasons: she was aware of time passing and her own mortality; she had bittersweet feelings about her son, who was living far from home; and she could no longer tolerate the greed, lying, and small-minded politics she encountered every day at her job.

And then she added a fourth reason - her disappointment at what she had failed to do in life. It's not that she'd wanted to be anything in particular, such as a doctor, a lawyer, a writer, or a leader of some kind. It was rather that she'd lived almost fifty years and had never really known what she wanted. Good things had happened to her, things for which she was grateful, but she'd always had the nagging feeling that there was something important she just wasn't getting to and that time was running out on some dream she couldn't even identify.

You can hear in this description the issue of meaning and purpose. Nancy was suffering from specific circumstances, but she was also feeling the absence of any organizing principle in her life. With this in mind, Nancy was guided into the transpersonal practice of **Inner Wisdom.**

PRACTICE 8: INNER WISDOM

Steps

1. Relax your shoulders, follow you breath, and let your body be held by your chair.

2. Begin to reflect on something you are wondering about at this point in your life... perhaps something about a decision you are trying to make... or something about yourself you are trying to understand better... or something about which you need guidance ...

3. Try to identify the question you are asking yourself. What's the question that gets to the heart of the matter? It's okay if you don't get it exactly.

4. And now turn your attention to the middle of your chest... and now, your mouth...and now, the sensation of breath passing through your nostrils... and now move your awareness all the way up to your left eye... and now your right eye... and now the space between your eyebrows... and now the middle of your forehead...

5. Now begin moving inside, into your imagination, and imagine a road or path stretching out in front of you... one you know or one you create... get a sense of walking on this path...

6. And begin to imagine, in the distance, a wise being, a wisdom figure, of any kind...any kind at all...coming toward you...

7. Ask your question…and be open to whatever happens to you…take as much time as you want…
8. When the inner experience fades, sit quietly and absorb its meaning for you.

Discussion. Sometimes, too much anxiety can block our mind and body to a crippling degree. We become incapable of taking a test, speaking in public, going to an interview, confronting the boss, dancing at a party, riding in an elevator, being in large crowds, traveling on airplanes, or looking down from heights. It was certainly possible that Nancy's anxiety might have blocked her from relaxing enough to benefit from the **Inner Wisdom** practice. In fact, her inner wisdom broke through into her consciousness at once.

When she was asked to picture in her imagination a wisdom figure or wise being of any kind, she saw a figure she described as a Chinese monk floating in the air over a deep valley. She then noticed an image of herself pinned in fear against the wall of a narrow mountain ledge overlooking the valley. She asked the wisdom figure about her fear. The monk responded by gesturing for her to leave the ledge and come out to join him in midair. Her reaction was to look down into the abyss of the deep valley and press herself even more desperately against the wall. The monk gestured again, but Nancy didn't move.

At that point she opened her eyes and asked in astonishment, "What the hell was that?"

In our years of working with people's imagination, we've come to understand that the images it presents to any particular person have meanings that are unique to that person. It's therefore inappropriate for us to make assumptions about what someone else's personal images might mean.

To find out more about the images she had seen, Nancy was asked to close her eyes again and recapture the image of the monk. Once she had done that, she was guided to use her creativity to imagine *becoming* the monk, to let her consciousness slip into his and to imagine what the world would look like and feel like if seen through his eyes.

She became silent and still, and then she said, "Oh, my God!"

Richard waited for Nancy to go through her experience. After about a minute, Nancy opened her eyes and said that she felt joy flowing through her body. She then sat quietly for several minutes taking in what she was experiencing. She didn't want to say anymore.

Before leaving the office, she was given the homework to write about her experience. This began Nancy's cultivation of a relationship to her inner wisdom.

When you have experiences like Nancy's, it is important to sit with them without rushing to give them words. You can trust that, later on, you will naturally feel the desire to give words to the experiences. Your mind will seek ways to give meaning to them because it knows that something new and of fundamental importance has happened to you.

Nancy had made direct conscious contact, perhaps for the first time in her life, with the transpersonal aspect of her nature. Initially, she was too fearful to let go of the mountainside - her instinctive, self-protective behaviors - and embrace the freedom personified by the monk. By allowing herself to imagine seeing the world through his eyes, she was able to feel, even for a moment, the joy that can come from living with a fearless consciousness.

Images of Inner Wisdom

Nancy's wisdom figure, which came to her spontaneously in the imagery practice, was a Chinese monk. There are countless varieties of wisdom figures that come up in clients' minds. A wise old man or a wise old woman is often a natural choice, sometimes related to loving memories of a grandfather or grandmother. Clients have also experienced a lotus, a rose, the sun, a room of light, an angel, a religious figure such as Jesus or Buddha, an ancient tree, a power animal, among almost countless others, as their wisdom figure.

These images can happen in combination. For example, some clients begin with imagining the bud of a rose that gradually opens, and then a spiritual teacher appears inside it.

Different wisdom figure images often emerge to communicate different kinds of information. One of our meditation students had been visualizing the image of a wooden statue of a seated monk, when, during one of her inner wisdom practices, the monk stood up, threw himself into a fire, and never came back. In the student's next practice, an old crone appeared as her image of wisdom.

Some of us do not have the visual imagination vivid enough to clearly see an inner image. Instead, you may hear inner words or feel a change of emotion or energy as you contact your inner wisdom. As you practice, you begin to learn the specific ways in which your inner wisdom comes to you and affects you. In time, you may find that you will notice the information from your inner wisdom without the need for any method or conscious effort. That is optimally the goal of the practice – to have access to your inner wisdom at any time.

Self-Practice with Inner Wisdom

The visualization of a wisdom figure is most useful when you need to know more about the direction of your life and the choices you are making for yourself. You can also ask your wisdom figure about deep doubts you might harbor about yourself or about spiritual or theological matters. The range of questions can be so broad because your inner wisdom, oriented around the purpose of your life, sees all questions as relevant to the proper use of your life energy.

You may want to try this practice first with a friend to guide you, or you could record the directions and be guided by your own voice. It is important to go slowly and be patient.

The practice may seem simple, but the answers you receive might surprise you. They may be one-word answers or long, elaborate inner visions. One man's inner wisdom image was a road and, no matter how long he kept walking on it in his imagination, he was getting nowhere. It immediately struck him that the pointless road was exactly the way his current life felt to him. Such information challenged him to look more carefully at the choices he was making.

The important thing is to return to the practice again and again and to keep a diary of your experiences. You will be gradually cultivating direct access to a deeper level of your mind.

Case Example: Hilda

It is a truth that even the most cynical among us can connect with our inner wisdom. One client who proved this truth was a 77 year old woman named Hilda who was facing a recurrence of breast cancer. Six years before, when she was first treated, her husband had been there to support her, but he had since died. Now, even though her doctor was optimistic about her prognosis, Hilda didn't think she would have the strength to go through treatment again on her own.

She told Bonney that the emptiness she felt in herself had become frightening. "I have no strong feelings, no delights, no disappointments," she said. "Nothing matters."

She then went on to say that as a young woman in Austria, she would face her problems by cutting herself off from the world and going "to a lonely place in the heather" to retreat into herself, contemplate, and figure out answers.

After listening to Hilda describing her despair, Bonney suggested that she close her eyes and relax. The intention was to guide her into an inner wisdom experience, but there was no need to suggest a wisdom figure. Hilda had already described an image for a source of answers - the heather.

She was asked to close her eyes and to allow herself to drift back in time, finding herself in the heather again, and be open to whatever happens.

This is how she later wrote about her meditative experience:

"I transported myself mentally to a suburban train heading to the heather. It's a beautiful summer day. The passing landscape is hazy, impressionistic. I get off at the heather station and walk down a long, gray, wide, very dusty road with deep ruts created by heavy wagons. There are no cars on this squalid road.

"There are hardly any people. A few old fenced-in farmhouses to the right and left. Maybe no one lives in them. I walk on and see a little side path leading directly to the heather. I take the path and after a while even that ends. I go on, slowing down because of the thickness of the heather, and continue through this unlimited, unending heather field broken by only a few birch trees. This is real wilderness without man's interference.

"Finally I sit down near some trees. How wonderful.

"I decide to lie down and look at the cloudless, silky, pale blue sky, draped like a dome over the horizon. A very gentle wind caresses me and makes the little gray-greenish leaves of the birches move slightly, maybe talking together about the intruder – me - who lies so motionless. A few butterflies flutter around, busy bees hum and collect the nectar from the flowers of the heather and move gracefully with the wind. Everything is peaceful and disconnected from the daily crazy world. What a glorious day!

"But I did not come here for adoration. I came to find my purpose, to feel better. I have to start searching. I fall into a deep sleep.

"I have to go down a chute, deep into the uncontrolled conflicts within me, past the vanity and finding excuses for everything I do, past the lies I tell myself, until I come to my own core, bare and naked, where my innermost soul begins.

I sink deeper into sleep.

"What is my problem? Is it the relationship between me and my family? Is it the relationship between friends and myself?

Why do I suffer so much defeat despite wanting success? What is the destructive chemistry inside me?

"I believe these are questions without easy answers. But to put the questions into words is already a cleansing, an awareness process.

"Slowly I begin to wake up from this kind of trance. My hair sticks to my face. I smell the strong, good, earthy soil on which I lie and I love it. The sun is high in the sky now. I feel sweaty but good about myself, and I start walking again. Far away I see a herd of sheep with a shepherd. When I pass him, we greet one another.

"Moving over this lovely, purplish, unending carpet of heather, I suddenly come to a big swimming pool filled with clear green water in the middle of nowhere. At the edge stands a short, white-haired, dark-skinned man who says hello. We talk a bit and he invites me to swim in his pool. I tell him I am a poor swimmer. I lose my breath easily from fear and would never let go of the ground beneath me.

"He finally persuades me to swim across by promising to jump in immediately if I lose my breath or get panicky. Somehow I trust him and slowly submerge myself in the clear water.

"Swim," he orders me. It is a command. I have to follow. I swim across, making sure he is still standing on the edge. I come to the far side of the pool and decide to stop.

"Turn and swim back—swim, swim. You can do it."

I listen to him and do the exercise several times without stopping. I never did such a long swim before in my life and I didn't have any breathing problems.

"Finally I get out of the water and can hardly believe it was me who accomplished all this swimming. What kind of man was he to give me all this unexpected power and confidence? I don't know. I never see him again.

This achievement on that day gave me such an immense, beyond-any-words feeling of happiness that I will and never could forget it. What a beautiful day!"

Somehow I trusted him and submerged myself in the clear water (Photo credits: George Schaub).

Discussion. Hilda was definitely not someone who would have believed in the concept of guiding inner wisdom. Her life experience, in fact, had taught her quite the opposite - that there was very little of positive value to be found in human nature. She probably could have filled an entire book with her negative opinions of religion, spirituality, and anything that sounded like them. And yet, despite her cynicism, Hilda clearly connected with her inner wisdom that day and derived great benefit from it. Through her experience, she felt a new curiosity about life and a belief in her own innate possibilities.

Ultimately, the experience is what gave her the strength to begin her cancer treatment.

Case Example: Clyde

Here is another inner wisdom discovery. Clyde had HIV-AIDS and was confined to his home. He was suffering too much neurological damage to go out. His skin itched severely from the side-effects of medication. (This took place before the advent of the more recent and more effective HIV-AIDS medications.)

He was angry that he was going to die soon, and on top of that he had to suffer the humiliation of dying from a socially-stigmatizing illness. Under these circumstances, it would be hard to imagine how a transpersonal breakthrough could happen or how it could help. In fact, a breakthrough happened that helped Clyde for the remaining months of his life.

On a home visit by a nurse trained in meditation and imagery, Clyde was guided into a variation of an **Inner Wisdom** meditation. He was asked to close his eyes and to follow his breathing. The nurse suggested that Clyde allow his breathing to be easy and without effort. He was then asked to imagine that each breath had the potential to take him deeper and deeper into calmness. (This is a standard relaxation practice in imagery and hypnosis.)

Clyde's chest went into a slower breathing pattern. He was experiencing a relaxed, inwardly absorbed state. The nurse then talked about the fact that in all times and in all cultures, people have prepared themselves for meditation in exactly the same way Clyde was now doing. The nurse spoke further about meditation as an ageless practice for realizing inner wisdom. The nurse then wondered out loud if Clyde could begin to notice someone in another time and place following his breath and preparing for inner wisdom, just as Clyde was doing now. The nurse said nothing more.

The rising and falling of Clyde's chest became very slow. The nurse felt a palpable peace in the room. Twenty minutes passed.

Clyde began to open his eyes. This is what happened to him in those twenty minutes:

"I felt my body sink deep in the bed. I felt a great heaviness and peace. The itching was gone, and it's still gone.

"I saw an image of a young man. I saw him become ill, and saw his flesh begin to fall off him, until he became a skeleton. Then his flesh came back to him, and his life force returned. He was the same healthy young man I first saw.

"Soon, the flesh began to come off him again, his life force left him, and he became a skeleton again. At that point, I saw an old man behind him. I realized that as the old man moved his hand to the left, the flesh came off the young man, and as the old man moved his hand to the right, the flesh came back to the young man.

"I watched this with great feelings of peace. I felt something very important was being taught to me. I can't even say the peace was in me, because by the time I was watching this I had absolutely no sense of my body at all. My body was gone. My body had dropped away. I was free, I was floating free. I had no fear at all. I was free."

Describing this, Clyde cried with happiness.

In her next visit, the visiting nurse met three of his friends sitting with him. Clyde asked the nurse to train the friends in the **Inner Wisdom** practice that had freed him. He wanted as many people as possible to be able to guide him into the meditation. He had found a way to break through his agony.

In a month, Clyde could no longer manage at home. He was hospitalized, and after a few days he stopped communicating. He was not in a coma, but his attention was definitely elsewhere. Visitors would talk to him, not get a reply, and then leave. When the nurse visited him in the hospital, the same thing happened. Everyone began to accept this as either a neurological and/or emotional consequence of his dying process.

One evening, his friend, Paul, was visiting at Clyde's hospital bed-side. As Paul stood up to leave, the floor nurse told Paul that this was probably Clyde's last night. Clyde's vital signs and her long clinical experience told her so. Paul became upset and started to go toward the elevator. He suddenly remembered a promise he'd made to Clyde - to guide him into the **Inner Wisdom** meditation in the event he was about to die.

Paul went back to the hospital room. There was Clyde, silent, unmov-ing. Feeling self-conscious, Paul leaned close to Clyde's ear and began to guide him into the **Inner Wisdom** practice. Clyde continued to lie there, unresponsive.

Paul finished the guiding. A few minutes later, Paul was surprised to see Clyde getting ready to speak. Paul leaned close. Clyde said, "Don't worry – Clyde's already gone."

Paul felt like laughing and crying. He didn't know what was happening to him. He felt the need to go outside for some fresh air. Clyde died a half hour later.

Discussion. It is not too much to claim that Clyde's suffering had been transformed in the last few weeks of his life into a spiritual journey and peaceful passing. The nurse's train-ing in the **Huntington Method** had been instrumental in that transformation.

The Availability of Inner Wisdom

The case examples of Nancy, Hilda and Clyde involve people in extremely difficult circumstances. We chose them to illustrate that transpersonal resources are available to clients at any time. It may even be that, under such difficult circumstances, the transpersonal aspect of your nature is easier to access because your personality has surrendered and has no answers. It does not, however, require such suffering in order to open to your deeper nature. Your inner wisdom is with you all the time and is potentially always available. The skill is to know how to gain access to it.

The next two practices, **Time of Meaning** and **Mountain Path**, also tap into your imagination to access guiding wisdom.

PRACTICE 9: TIME OF MEANING

Steps

1. Make your body comfortable…Let the chair hold you… lower or close your eyes…
2. Now follow your breathing…don't do anything to your breathing…just let it be…just notice it…
3. And now let your awareness go into your mind…and into your memory…and let a time come to you when you felt a sense of meaning and purpose in your life…a

sense of wholeness…let the details begin to come to you…

4. And now begin to realize what the essence of that time was…What was at the heart of it for you? Take your time…

Wait three minutes and then say, "And now let go of the practice and turn your attention to noticing how you are…"

Wait thirty seconds and then say, "And when you feel ready, at your own pace, begin to come back to the room…"

Case Study: Tim

Tim was a war veteran in his 40s who felt he had never re-joined "normal" life after his Army service was over. He was in despair. He was stuck in a directionless inner struggle with himself and his place in the world. Asked about a time when he felt his life mattered, he couldn't think of anything. The **Time of Meaning** meditation and imagery practice gave him a clear answer.

In the meditation, he saw memories of being taught how to scuba dive by a veteran buddy of his. He remembered the moments going down, down, down, eventually into the blackness of deep water. He was alert and totally focused on the sounds of his breathing as he penetrated into the darkness.

The end of the dive was a slow climb upward into the increasing brightness of the sunlit ocean. He described the thrill he felt at the end of those dives. They were "real" because they brought him into direct contact with the truth of the fragility of life.

Discussion. The memory evoked by the **Time of Meaning** practice totally surprised Tim. He would never have thought that the scuba diving memories held such important information for him. He understood that, despite periods when he feels like giving up, he does want to get back into the light. In contact with his inner wisdom, he was being guided to shift his focus from his despair to his deeper desire to be here and to live a life that matters. This is the life-affirming aspect of your inner wisdom and its orientation around your life purpose.

PRACTICE 10: MOUNTAIN PATH

This is another transpersonal practice designed to tap into your guiding inner wisdom. Executive coach Whitmore found this particularly useful with his clients.

Steps

1. Allow the chair to hold you…
2. Now begin to notice the sensations in the middle of your chest…your throat…and now to your nostrils and your

breath…and now moving your awareness all the way up to your left eye…and now your right eye…and now the space between your eyebrows…

3. And now begin moving into your imagination, imagining that you are standing at the bottom of a mountain…one you know or one you create…

4. And now imagine a path that goes from the bottom to the top…and now step on that path, feeling yourself going up…

5. Along the path, you will find something you need… When you find it, take it with you to the top…

6. Up at the top, there's place for you to sit…You can see across the mountain range in all directions…And now let your intuition begin to tell you about what you found on the path…

Wait one minute and then say, "And now let go of the practice and turn your attention to noticing how you are…"

Wait thirty seconds and then say, "And when you feel ready, at your own pace, begin to come back to the room…"

Discussion. The **Mountain Path** practice is of course an imagined scene, but it is drawing upon the same process as the **Inner Wisdom** and **Time of Meaning** practices. In each of them, you are entering a meditative state and then asking a question in your imagination to see what it stimulates. The use of the imagination is very specifically chosen because it is the creative, intuitive aspect of your mind.

In the **Mountain Path** practice, you are asking your imagination to show you "something you need." It is a vague request and leaves it wide open to the creative, intuitive mind to provide an answer.

Two client examples follow. In both cases, the clients felt stuck, undergoing variations on the mid-life crisis described earlier in the book.

Halfway up the mountain path, Damien found a small box. He then got back on the path to the top. Sitting up there, looking out at the vast vista of the mountain range, he realized that the box symbolized how "small" he keeps himself. He hides his emotions, he doesn't admit to his ambitions, he doesn't act on any of his creative ideas.

These realizations may at first sound negative, but Damien took great comfort in the fact that the wisdom was clear and true. He knew exactly what it was saying to him. He was also fascinated by the mysterious process by which his imagination organized and presented such wisdom. The experience felt reassuring because something beyond his "stuckness" was active in him and trying to guide him.

Halfway up the mountain path, Linda found an old man sitting in a cabin throwing ashes on the flames in the fireplace. It seemed an odd thing for Linda to have to get back on the path and resume her climb to the top while dragging the old man, the cabin, and the fireplace with her, but she did so. In the vastness of the imagination, anything can happen and anything can be done.

When she got to the mountaintop and let her intuition tell her about her symbol, she immediately understood that she throws ashes on her own fire, on her own passion for life. Memories flashed by her in which she chose conformity over what she really cares about. Sitting on that imaginal mountaintop, she vowed that she would go for woodworking training which she had always respected and had been artistically drawn to do. As with Damien, Linda was intrigued by the fact that some part of her mind had organized these images and memories for her.

Clients are intrigued by the realization that there are deeper processes going on in them which they can discover and benefit from. Transpersonal development is an education about the ignored resources in every one of us.

As we've said earlier, part of the power of the transpersonal level of your mind is the surprise element. Clients are intrigued by the realization that there are deeper processes going on in them which they can discover and benefit from. Transpersonal development is an education about the ignored resources in every one of us.

The **Mountain Path** practice is a metaphor for discovery. There are many similar metaphors which involve going to a new place and discovering new insights about your life. The mountain path metaphor could be replaced by going down a hallway and opening a door, walking in dark woods and coming to a sunlit clearing, entering a cave and shining light into the darkness, and many other examples.

Three Features of Inner Wisdom Experience

When you enter *unfocused* into your imagination, a wide and wild range of images and thoughts can come to you. But when you enter the imagination *focused* and holding a question in mind, creative, intuitive answers such as Damien's small box and Linda's ashes on the flame come forward.

The doubt then naturally rises: how can you trust that the imagined information is actually wise and worthy of your consideration? Surely, there are fears and negative scenarios in your imagination that you would not want to follow as guidance. In addition, there is the concern that you are just making up these images and imbuing them with meaning that they don't deserve.

When you enter the imagination focused, creative, intuitive answers emerge (Photo credits: George Schaub).

Over our years of transpersonal practice, we have seen three features which characterize trustworthy inner wisdom:

- **Surprise.** The information shows you a new way to grasp a situation or question. It opens and expands your thinking.
- **Peace and relief.** The information feels true, and the truth relaxes you.
- **Gratitude.** The information makes you feel grateful that this wise part of you actually exists.

The small box and ashes on the flame are not symbols that either client would have deliberately conjured up. The symbols came to them, and the meanings were understandable and relevant to their lives. The mystery becomes one of wondering what part of their nature generated these wise symbols and what part of them understood them immediately. And what is this guiding wisdom trying to accomplish?

As you become a student of the wisdom inside you, you realize that it is directing you toward your third transpersonal quality – *life purpose.*

Life Purpose

"In contrast to religious or philosophical meaning, which can change over time, individual human meaning remain permanent." —VIKTOR FRANKL

Hope is the energy of life. If you have hope, or regain hope, you get a renewal of energy. If, on the other hand, you think hopelessly, the result is that you feel no energy for living.

Hopelessness has been identified as a chief characteristic and possible cause of depression. When cognitive behavioral therapists help people to change their hopeless thinking, the clients' depressions often lift. The mind's energy, if linked to hopelessness, physiologically depresses the central nervous system. The reversal of that thinking - the linking of your mind's energy to hope - rallies your central nervous system. This is not necessarily easy to do. Some life situations feel so sad and hopeless that it takes a long time for hope to be possible again.

It is with these crucial facts about hope that we approach our next practice.

PRACTICE 11: HOPE/DEEPER HOPE

Steps

1. Make your body comfortable and let the chair hold you... lower or close your eyes...

2. Now follow your breathing...don't do anything to it... just let it be the way it is...you're just noticing it...

3. In a moment, I'm going to ask you to ask yourself two questions. When you ask the first question, try not to think up the answer. Just ask the question and be open to whatever comes to you. If nothing comes to you, that's fine...then we'll go on to the second question...

4. Now, for a moment, go back to your breath...

5. And now ask yourself this question...just be open to what comes to you...Here's the question: "In the way that my life is going now, what am I hoping for?"

6. Pause 30 seconds and then say, "And now let yourself go deeper and ask yourself: 'What is my deeper hope'?"

Wait two minutes and then say, "And now let go of the practice and turn your attention to noticing how you are..."

Wait thirty seconds and then say, "And when you feel ready, at your own pace, begin to come back to the room..."

Discussion If you were asked about your hope and deeper hope, you would *think* of answers. But when you enter the meditative state and ask the same questions, answers come to you from your guiding inner wisdom. Creative, intuitive answers include but go beyond rational thought.

The next practice builds on this principle.

PRACTICE 12:
INTENTION MEDITATION

This practice flows directly from the **Hope** meditation. Once you can identify your deeper hope, you want to energize and cultivate it. To do so, we use the **Intention Meditation.**

The actual steps of the **Intention Meditation** resemble self-hypnosis. Other terms for this are self-suggestion, self-talk, psychological feeding, affirmation, and vision statements. The goal is to give your mind a frequent diet of your intended hope so that you are more fully alert to acting on it in your choices and behaviors.

As one case example, a depressed businessman had stopped taking anti-depressant medication and wanted to find an alternative way to re-energize his life. The **Hope** meditation was revealing. His hope was to get more customers, but his deeper hope was *to truly help people.*

This second answer surprised him because he would not have consciously thought of it. In the meditative state, however, it came to him immediately, and he knew exactly what it meant. He had been successful in his business dealing with people, but he felt no sense of real contribution or purpose. His inner wisdom told him he would feel a renewed sense of hope if he was *truly* helping people. This meant to him that he would *truly* assess customers' needs to see if they really needed his product and services. He would take care of his customers as he would wish to be taken care of. This would be his new contribution and purpose everyday.

With this man's example in mind, we will go through the steps of the **Intention Meditation.**

Steps

1. Let the chair hold you and lower or close your eyes…
2. Now begin to notice your breathing in your nostrils, your chest, or your belly…wherever it is easiest to notice… don't do anything to your breathing…just let it be…just notice it…
3. Remembering your intention – *I will truly help people* - begin to link that statement to your in-breath…each time you feel the in-breath, say your intention in your mind… and then breath out normally…

Wait two minutes and then say, "And now let go of the practice and turn your attention to noticing how you are…"

Wait thirty seconds and then say, "And when you feel ready, at your own pace, begin to come back to the room…"

Discussion. This is a quietly powerful practice. It can be done anytime, anywhere, and is effective even if done for just a few minutes. In our case example, the client did this on his coffee breaks at work. He began to really like doing it because it calmed him down and made him feel better about himself: in others words, it gave him hope.

A startling development occurred as he used this practice over the course of a month. He began to get very busy. New customers were calling him without any new advertising or outreach on his part. When he asked the callers why they were getting in touch with him, he was told that they'd had his name for months or even a year but somehow felt that *now was the time to call.*

This coincidence between his **Intention Meditation** and his sudden increase in business, providing him with the opportunity *to truly help people*, is a curiosity. There are theories - intentionality, positive thinking, the power of prayer - about such possible interactions between your mind and other people. The theories suggest that your mind is a kind of transmitter and receiver that can link to other people's minds, and that a powerful positive thought sent by you is received by others. Briefly stated, this possibility is based on the concept that the universe is an energetic field and that thought is capable of travelling in the universal energetic field. Did the client's intentions travel into the minds of his new customers who somehow felt that *now was the time to call*?

While such theories are beyond the scope of this book, they are a fascinating subject to explore (see, for example, Dossey, 1994; 2009; 2013). For our purposes, the practice helped to re-energize this client's sense of purpose and gave him the opportunity to truly help people.

In terms of staying true to your life purpose, the use of the **Intention Meditation** is not a luxury. It is a necessity. Your mind is filled with all manner of impulses, half-baked ideas and future-oriented scenarios. Your life purpose can get easily lost in that forest of mental activities. Adding to the confusion, you must cope with the negative opinions you have memorized about yourself and all of the worries and warnings sent to you by the fear-based aspect of your brain. It is not an easy task for your life purpose to receive the focused mental energy it requires for you to act on it. Without a deliberate meditative practice to energize your life purpose in your mind, it can deteriorate into a wish you can't even remember.

In terms of staying true to your life purpose, the use of the Intention Meditation is not a luxury. It is a necessity. Your mind is filled with all manner of impulses, half-baked ideas and future-oriented scenarios. Your life purpose can get easily lost in that forest of mental activities.

Oneness

"Spiritual realization is the direct experience of the part of your nature that is identical to the great energy pervading the universe."

—ROBERTO ASSAGIOLI

Of all the scientific fields that support transpersonal development, brain imaging research is of special importance. Using SPECT (Single Photon Emission Computed Tomography), we can photograph the brain in different states of experience (Newberg & D'Aquila, 2001). SPECT imaging can visually document the dramatic differences between our brain in a state of fear and our brain in a state of meditation.

By itself, this is beneficial because we can determine which practices cause positive changes in the brain. But neurologists Newberg and D'Aquili went further, much further. They reported that there is a dormant region of the brain which, when activated, opens us to a state of loving oneness with all of life, a state which Newberg and D'Aquili termed *absolute unitary being (AUB)*. They hypothesized that *AUB* may be the condition that different religions call heaven, nirvana, or paradise—by any name, the ultimate experience of human life. Similarly, Austin charted the neurological course that unfolds through Zen meditation toward an enlightened state of *oneness* (Austin, 2006). In the words of one journalist investigating brain research, David Brooks of the New York Times: "These moments of elevated experience happen when we step outside our separated boundaries and overflow with love" (2011). These brain states and experiences go beyond the personality, i.e., they are transpersonal.

Feeling at one with the "great energy pervading the universe" is a life-changing moment. Assagioli personally knew the *AUB* experience well, which is why he wrote the word *Joy!* all over his diaries and journals. The way to experience this uniting of energies, this loving oneness, is through awareness itself.

The Three Forms of Awareness. Along with transpersonal development specialist Michael Follman (2012), we identify three conditions of awareness itself:

- **Attending** – when your awareness is *paying attention to something in particular*, whether it be a thought, a sensation, an external experience. In our transpersonal practices, examples of attending are **Let Go, Body Scan, Centering, Pain Management** and **Intention Meditation.**
- **Receiving** – when your awareness is in *an open observing state, noticing and receiving* whatever comes to you.

Examples are **Stream of Consciousness, Centering and Naming, Defeating Difficult Thoughts, Inner Wisdom, Time of Meaning, Mountain Path** and **Hope**.

- **Uniting** - when your personal awareness feels *united with an energy-awareness greater than yourself.* **Awareness Itself** and **Center of Awareness** are designed to guide you toward this uniting experience.

The Availability of Oneness

Enlightened states of being are associated with mystics, poets, and saints. In fact, the realization of oneness is available to each person without exception because each person is already participating in it.

What are we all participating in? The non-visible pervading creative energy that animates all of life. This energy has been directly experienced by people in every time and culture. It has been variously called universal chi, ki, prana, holy spirit, the Source, the Divine, the One Mind, underlying implicate order, the fabric of reality, the energetic field, awareness of awareness, the Self, ground of being, subtle energy, and many other terms.

In moments of oneness, your consciousness temporarily and joyfully merges into the universal pervading energy and has the instantaneous knowing that this is the source of all that is. In some instances with seriously ill clients, the experience of oneness has wiped away the fear of death. It provides reassurance that you are intimately involved in something far greater than yourself.

After the Florentine poet Dante entered into oneness, he put it this way:

> "I felt my will and my desire impelled by the Love
> that moves the sun and other stars."

Oneness calms your self-referential survival fears. Instinctual anxiety is replaced by transpersonal joy.

PRACTICE 13: AWARENESS ITSELF

You experience your mind most of all when you are thinking. It would be easy to conclude that your mind and thinking are synonymous. Much of your thinking, however, is a mixture of half-thoughts, images, phrases, self-criticisms, chatter, narratives, fictions, fantasies, urges, etc. If our minds are to be defined by the thinking process, we're all in a lot of trouble.

Fortunately, thinking is not the essential nature of your mind. Your mind's true nature is the energy of awareness itself.

Awareness is primary, experience is secondary. Without awareness, you would have no experience at all. Awareness makes experience possible. Life itself only exists for you because you have awareness. When someone blacks out or goes under anesthesia, they have no experience. When they are aware again, they have experience. Awareness is the basis of your experience. Your mind's most essential state is awareness itself in which thinking is one of the many activities you notice.

Steps

1. Settle yourself in your chair and lower or close your eyes…

2. Now begin by listening…(Pause about 20 seconds)

3. Now begin to notice your body in the chair… (20 seconds)

4. Now begin to notice your mood, your feelings… (20 seconds)

5. Now begin to notice the sensations of your face…now, within your face, your mouth…now your nostrils and breath…

6. And now move your awareness to your left eye…sensations of your left eye…and now over to your right eye…

7. And now move awareness to the space between your eyebrows…

8. You have just moved your awareness from listening…
   to your body…to your mood…to your face…to your
   mouth, your breath, your eyes, and to the space between
   your eyebrows…

9. Now see if you can sense and feel this awareness itself
   that you have been moving through you…

Wait two minutes and then say, "And now let go of the practice and turn your attention to noticing how you are…"

Wait thirty seconds and then say, "And when you feel ready, at
your own pace, begin to come back to the room…"

Discussion. While you are always changing, awareness is always the same. It is awareness itself that gives you the continuous experience of always being here and always being
yourself even when you're going through changes.

This unique quality of awareness has led many spiritual traditions to investigate its true nature. The Vedanta tradition of
Hinduism and the Dzogchen ("the ultimate practice") tradition in Tibetan Buddhism are two examples.

In Vedanta, the entire universe is energy which is aware. The
direct experience of this is called *satchitananda*: sat is being, chit is knowledge of truth, ananda is bliss. The respected Tibetan Buddhist teacher, Dudjom Rinpoche, counsels

students to *know the one thing that liberates everything - awareness itself* (Bauer, 2011).

From this perspective, awareness is not produced by your brain or body and is not limited to your brain or body. Rather, you are participating in an all-pervading, interpenetrating field of universal energy which is aware.

In the course of these transpersonal practices, you should be mindful that clients have the possibility of experiencing the liberating energy of awareness itself. If they do so, they may not have the language for it. You can have the language, however: you can tell them that they just had a moment of transpersonal discovery.

Case Study: Eileen

Eileen came to meditation class to reduce her anxiety, which was based on the cold reality that she had a debilitating and possibly fatal illness. Her motivation was very strong, and she came to every class ready to give herself over to the meditative state. After three months, she had a breakthrough experience.

She was in class meditating on awareness itself when suddenly she began to experience her whole body as an energy field. Then she felt her awareness expanding to experience the whole meditation classroom as an energy field.

Eileen's awareness kept expanding and expanding until it took in the whole city, then the land and water surrounding the city, and finally the whole planet. Eileen experienced the whole planet as an energy field with her awareness distributed everywhere throughout the field. She could see in every direction and she was pervaded with a dancing joy. Time was gone. Confinement in the body was gone. Eileen, as she had previously defined Eileen, was gone.

When Eileen re-emerged into awareness of the meditation class a few seconds later, her feeling of joy took in the entire the room and all people in it. All the colors were vibrant masterpieces, all the objects perfect. She was experiencing the aftermath of her oneness experience, floating on a sea of gratitude.

The class ended and Eileen started toward home. As she walked, she sensed she had just been changed forever. Over the next few days, the changes kept coming to her. She no longer felt afraid of death. She now felt curious about it. But, at the same time, she also loved life more than she ever had before the breakthrough and was in no hurry to die.

Her mind had a new clarity and peace. She could pay deeper attention to her work and her friends. She could see other people's viewpoints completely and felt no attachment to arguing with them because she found it much more satisfying to whole-heartedly try to understand them. And she found that when she tried to communicate her understanding of their view, people more easily let go of their view to ask about hers. This new way of being became so noticeable at work that her boss began to ask her to handle negotiations with the most difficult clients.

She could walk down a street and unexpectedly be in bliss at all of the richness and variety of life. Her understanding of God changed from what had been a non-credible super-being in the sky to a limitless inter-penetrating spirit of love and order that was present here and now. This new understanding simply showed up in her mind one day without conscious effort, and it gave her the equanimity to face her illness.

PRACTICE 14: CENTER OF AWARENESS

This practice helps you to identify with the centrality of awareness in your life.

Steps

1. Close your eyes…let the chair hold you…drop your shoulders…

2. Find your breath, either in your nose, your chest, or your belly…begin to tune into your breath…

3. Leaving some of your attention on your breath, bring the rest of your attention into your mind, and in there say to yourself slowly several times, "I have feelings, and I am more than my feelings…" (Pause 30 seconds)

4. And now say to yourself several times, "I have a mind, and I am more than my mind…" (Pause 30 seconds)

5. And now say to yourself several times, "I have a body, and I am more than my body…" (Pause 30 seconds)

6. And now say to yourself several times, "I am a center of awareness…" (Pause 30 seconds)

7. And now, begin to link the phrase "I am a center of awareness" to each in-breath, and then breathe out normally. Try this for a while…

Wait one minute and then say, "And now notice how you are…"

Wait one minute and then say, "And now, at your own pace, begin to return to the room and open your eyes."

Discussion. Sometimes clients feel baffled by this meditation. Any of us can become completely identified with our feelings, mind, and body as who we are - and of course they are very real. But, equally real, is your awareness itself. As we've discussed, you only have the experience of your feelings, mind and body because you have awareness. Awareness precedes experience. This practice helps you to identify with awareness itself as your own true, continuous nature while everything else in you and around you is changing.

PART THREE:

Transpersonal
Experiences

We started this book together with the goal of helping you and your clients to discover transpersonal resources. We took you through step-by-step practices to assist the discovery process. And, despite the neglect in our professional education about the transpersonal, we have asserted that the transpersonal part of your nature is objective fact. The most convincing proof will always be your own direct, personal experience.

The Three Features of Transpersonal Experience

There are three general features that characterize a transpersonal experience:

1. You experience an energetic/emotional shift that is new to you.
2. You simultaneously experience a knowing, a new understanding.
3. You feel you have just participated in something greater than yourself.

The overall impression of such an experience is that *it happens to you*, rather than that you caused it to happen. Even if you are praying, meditating, or otherwise engaged in a transpersonal practice, the specifics of the experience itself are not anything you create. One client, while meditating, described that he suddenly felt that he was "in a presence that included me." It was deeply peaceful and reassuring, and yet he had not tried to have such an experience. He would not even have known how to imagine being *in a presence that includes me*. It had simply happened to him.

The Varieties of Transpersonal Experience

These are some of the ways people have described their transpersonal experiences:

- a quiet joy pervading all things
- the delight of beauty
- feeling loving unity with all beings
- an instantly understood inner vision, an illumination
- feeling an extraordinary inner silence
- feeling contact with the soul
- inflows of inspiration
- equanimity
- freedom from self-conscious fears
- emotional expansiveness, laughing in a very deep way
- feeling again the mystery of life
- compassion and connection
- a sudden and important creative breakthrough
- liberation from the fear of death
- a "psychic" experience that causes awe
- a deep feeling of gratefulness

- moved by the wonder of life
- awareness as endless, boundless
- a clear sense of inner guidance
- awareness of awareness
- awareness of other lives in other places
- loving all persons in one person
- feeling oneself to be the channel for a stronger force to flow through
- only bliss everywhere
- merging with a work of art and the artist's intention

If a pill could give any of us these experiences, it would sell in the billions. The fact that a part of your nature can give you these experiences is a great motivation to find out more about them. It especially calls upon you as a helping professional, whose job it is to find answers to your clients' suffering, to investigate the methods which cultivate transpersonal experiences.

If a pill could give any of us these experiences, it would sell in the billions. The fact that a part of your nature can give you these experiences is a great motivation to find out more about them.

An intriguing place to start is the example of people who, with no method of any kind, *spontaneously* discovered their resources for peace, wisdom, purpose and oneness. The spontaneous discoveries matter because they remind you that transpersonal resources are already present inside each person who comes to you for help, and that your role is merely to find the right method that may open them to their transpersonal nature. A transpersonal method doesn't cause a transpersonal experience to take place – it invites it.

Spontaneous Experiences

A tired business executive went out into his suburban backyard at night and looked up at the stars. He suddenly felt an "energy" come down into him, and he went into a state of blissful oneness. He felt connected and in love with everything. (In the words of the brain researchers Newberg and D'Aquili, he was having a taste of *absolute unitary being*.)

The feeling lasted a few minutes and then began to fade, but an afterglow was still with him when he went back into the house. He told his wife about the experience, she called it weird, and they said no more about it.

Three years later, attending a seminar on meditation, he approached Richard after class and described his backyard experience. Richard was the second person he'd ever told. For

The spontaneous opening of the mind and heart (Photo credits: George Schaub).

three years, the man had lived in silence with an experience that he described as *other than the birth of my kids, it was the most important thing that's ever happened to me.* He wondered how it he could have it again.

A spontaneous, momentary transpersonal experience can have a lasting emotional effect. C.S. Lewis (1966), experiencing a sudden enormous joy while walking in an English garden, described his discovery in a way similar to our business executive:

> "It had taken only a moment of time; and in a certain sense everything else that had ever happened to me was insignificant in comparison" (1966, pp. 15-16).

Lewis goes on to describe a longing that the experience created in him:

> "...I doubt whether anyone who has tasted it would ever... exchange it for all the powers in the world...I call it joy... Joy...has indeed one characteristic...the fact that anyone who has experienced it will want it again" (pp. 15-16).

Some people become so inspired that they must pass the experience on to others. Two dramatic historical examples are Saul of Tarsus and Bill Wilson.

Saul, a 1st Century soldier and persecutor of the early followers of Jesus, was on the road to Damascus when he went into a state of bliss and oneness: "I was caught up in heaven…whether in the body or not, I do not know" (Bible, English Standard Version, 2001, 2 Corinthians 12:3). It completely re-oriented his life. He went on to become St. Paul, a prime figure in changing the then-obscure Christian sect into a worldwide religion.

Bill Wilson, a 20th Century hopeless middle-aged alcoholic, was admitted to the hospital for his fourth detoxification (Alcoholics Anonymous, 1984). Lying on his hospital bed, he was engulfed in a white light and a feeling of ecstasy. He instantaneously knew he was "a free man" and never drank again. He went on to co-found the 12 Steps of Alcoholics Anonymous, probably the 20th Century's most influential health movement that has saved hundreds of thousands of lives from the disease of alcoholism.

Longing

Transpersonal discoveries are much more than positive one-time events. A transpersonal experience sets a process in motion. Once you have discovered your deeper nature, you are naturally drawn to know more. The transpersonal development specialist Michael Follman (Schaub & Follman, 1996) highlights the process set in motion by transpersonal experiences:

- Something new has happened.
- Something of fundamental importance has happened.

- There are no memories to compare this experience to.

- The experience is its own immediate memory.

- The experience means more than can be presently understood.

- There is a desire to be true to the experience, to affirm it, to somehow protect it.

- There is a reticence about telling anyone who might question and judge the experience.

- There is the sense that the experience connected you to something greater than yourself, and there is a longing for more connection.

- The longing feels like it is for home, not the household home, but a deeper "being home."

- The longing for "home" feels completely true - you just need a way to find it. This gives a sense of destiny to the longing – you know you are supposed to do something with this new experience.

Transpersonal Paths

Whether it's in a suburban backyard, an English garden, on the road to Damascus, or in an alcohol detoxification unit, transpersonal experiences wait to be awakened inside each of us. To bring these possibilities and benefits into the helping professions, we have trained nurses, physicians, psychologists, psychotherapists, physical and occupational therapists, guidance counselors, clergy, human resource specialists, chiropractors, educators, addiction counselors and others in the **Huntington Method**.

We have emphasized meditation and imagery practices because they can be done in the office, the clinic, the hospital room, the classroom, the workplace - but such practices are only one path to the transpersonal. Our interviews with hundreds of clients over many years tell us that many people have their first transpersonal experiences through engagement with a work of art or in service to others. Additional paths to the transpersonal include devotion, social action, study and knowledge, ceremony, and physical training.

We will describe these paths to transpersonal experience in some detail. The practical purpose is for you to recognize the different ways that clients seek, consciously or unconsciously, to open themselves to their transpersonal nature. By identifying the paths that have affected them in the past, you can encourage them to re-visit those paths again. In our descriptions of the various paths, you may also recognize your own history of paths - and the current one you may be walking on now without even realizing it.

The Path of the Arts

Case Study: Miriam

Miriam was a 66 year old woman who had started drinking heavily after the death of her husband ten years ago. Up until that time, she had been a social drinker. She told her physician about her problem drinking, and he suggested that she go to Alcoholics Anonymous.

She had difficulty participating in AA. She was very turned off by the talk of God. She said she was not at all interested in religion or spirituality. Instead of AA, she consulted Bonney about getting help with her drinking through psychotherapy.

In taking her history, it turned out that Miriam did a lot of traveling after her husband's death. She used a large portion of her limited funds to do this.

She went to France and sought out Gothic cathedrals. She adored the stained glass windows, especially the rose windows. As her eyes stayed focused on the rosy light, she felt a quiet joy.

She traveled to India, not on a tour but on her own, because there were very particular sites she wanted to visit. These were places she had seen pictures of in books, especially an island where there were caves filled with Buddha statues. It wasn't easy to get to this island, and she had to arrange for a young guide to bring her there. Sitting in the caves, she felt a deep love for the sculptors of these statues and a deep respect for their dedication to create art that, many years after their deaths, would cause such peaceful feelings in future visitors like herself.

In expressing her admiration, she was quick to say it was purely on an aesthetic level. It had nothing to do with the spirituality of the places. She seemed embarrassed that she might sound like she was interested in such matters. Just as in her negative reaction to AA's spirituality, she cringed whenever she heard anything that sounded "spiritual."

Discussion. You can listen to Miriam and hear the quest of a woman searching for something beyond herself, something transpersonal. She had clearly felt in the French cathedral and the Indian cave the three features of a transpersonal experience – an energetic/emotional shift, a new knowing, a participation in something greater than herself.

Through the path of art, Miriam's deeper hope and her intention were clear. She wanted to experience herself as more than a 66 year old widow with a low mood and a drinking problem. She wanted inspiration and the courage to live the rest of her life with hope. Art was her path to her transpersonal nature.

Artistic inspiration. Assagioli spoke of artistic inspiration as a downflow of essential insight about reality into our conscious awareness and then expressing that insight through some form of art.

The classical music conductor Leonard Bernstein wrote about this surrendering to the downflow through his experience leading an orchestra:

> "...it takes minutes before I know where I am - in what concert hall, in what country, or who I am. It's a sort of ecstasy..."

Surely in your memory there are outstanding moments when a film, painting, photographic image, dance performance, poem, piece of music, architectural space or sculpture took you into the "downflow" of inspiration. Those are always the most outstanding artistic experiences. The downflow moves you toward the resource of oneness in your transpersonal nature.

Probably one of the great disappointments in any artistic offering is that something about it does not allow you to be moved by it. Perhaps it is too unreal or stupid or cliché-ridden, but the result is that you can't surrender to it. Instead, you sit there separated from the work and absorbed by your own habitual self.

Case Study: Laurie

One of Bonney's clients, Laurie, made diary notes about oneness while traveling in Rome. You can think of her experience as both spontaneous and deliberate. She deliberately traveled to a place filled with inspiration, but her transpersonal experience came to her as a surprise:

"Entering St. Peter's. Experiencing its hugeness. Awesome. Is this structure designed to humble me? I experience myself resisting it. All vertical and overbearing. I feel like I'm in the land of giants. There is beauty present, but it feels remote and cold. Perhaps when it is filled with thousands of worshippers, it will warm up and soften.

I find myself drawn to the side chapel where Michelangelo's Pieta is displayed. I can't approach it - it is behind a glass wall, protected from any threat of attack. It draws my gaze, despite the barrier, and I feel myself pulled towards it. I'm first drawn to the Virgin Mary's face. It is the face of a young girl not older than adolescent. Soft, delicate, yet serenely sad, wise beyond her years, yet innocent and confused by the situation she is in.

My eyes survey the rest of the sculpture. The soft, translucent white of the marble, the folds of drapery and the large figure of the dead Christ draped across Mary's lap. This lifeless body is much too large to be Mary's child. I've seen many Pietas - paintings and sculptures - why are there tears in my eyes? I'm drawn back to Mary's delicate face. I can't turn away. Why is she so young and innocent? Certainly Michelangelo knew how to sculpt an older woman. No, there is a reason she appears like this. Suddenly I understand. This image is about a human experience. Mary is a mother whose child has been killed. Is a person ever old enough to not be completely vulnerable to this loss?

When I first became a mother, I remember being frightened by the intensity of my protective instincts and the degree to which thoughts of my son being harmed terrified me. I feel joined to Mary's face. I can see myself and all mothers. My tears continue. The image expands to connecting with the universal fear of death and loss. Can my spirituality offer me solace in the face of this? Isn't loss one of the primary facts that draws us to a spiritual path? I think about how angry I get when I hear pat answers to the question, 'Why?' Don't tell me about karma, or God's Will, or that it's part of a lesson. Those answers bypass the sorrow, my experience of grief. This sculpture before me honors this. Somehow that look of innocence is even more compelling than if Mary's face had appeared ravaged and racked with sorrow. She needs compassion. She needs me to accompany her, be present with her. This allows me to gain strength from the shared human experience. I am not alone.

In this moment, I understand the power of the creative moment to transcend time and space - to draw me through the act of creation to a place of truth. Michelangelo was only 25 when he created this work. What did he know? I've lived twice as many years as he had - yet the place from which his genius and inspiration comes is timeless and universal. It emerges from the ground of being and includes me in it."

The world's spiritual traditions certainly recognize the power of the path of art. The greatest architecture, paintings, frescoes, and sculptures have all been created for and inspired by spiritual and religious feeling. The poets of transpersonal wisdom, including the author of the biblical Psalms, the German poet, Rainer Maria Rilke, the Sufi philosopher-poet, Rumi, the Italian mystic poet Dante, and many others, can offer just the right phase to suddenly cause a transpersonal opening in you.

The devotional music of the world, both traditional and modern, also provides doorways to transpersonal experience. Meditative and sacred music is designed for this very purpose, but certain popular music can also open you to a loving oneness with greater reality. In some pieces, the musician sounds as if he/she is in an inspired state. In other works, it is the musical mixture of the tones and pacing that link to your physiology and take you to a deeper state of peace.

The Path of Service

The quality of mercy is not strained,

It droppeth as the gentle rain from heaven

Upon the place beneath. It is twice blessed:

It blesseth him that gives and him that takes.

—SHAKESPEARE

We have trained hundreds of health professionals internationally in the clinical applications of meditation and imagery, and we have heard many stories of transpersonal experiences taking place during the course of their service to others in hospitals, clinics, and private practices. We often get the feeling that there is a mystical underground in the health professions (especially among nurses) because of their openness to the transpersonal.

Service generates transpersonal experience because it asks you to quiet your usual mind and body and to turn awareness fully toward another person, to accept them as they are, to let go of judgments, to imagine what it must be like for them. In other words, you are called upon to practice purpose and oneness every hour of the day. Every time you do this, you increase the possibility of the direct experience of your own transpersonal resources. You may be giving to another, but you are also the one receiving. As it says in the Bible, "Give and you shall receive."

Dramatic examples of people on this path, such as the founder of modern nursing, Florence Nightingale (Dossey, 2010), can often inspire acts of service in the rest of us, expanding the number of us taking ethical and loving actions in the world.

You don't need to be in a professional role to be on the path of service. It is a matter of how you treat others in any circumstances of your daily life. You can, for example, express kindness, with amazing results, while you are ordering a sandwich or buying a newspaper. Bonney found this out when she was riding home on a bus after her nursing shift.

She had witnessed a lot of suffering on the hospital unit that day, and she was in a distressed mood. Sitting in front of the bus going home, her mind was upset, and her body was agitated. After a few moments, the bus came to the next stop, and the driver lowered the bus to allow an elderly man with a cane to get onboard. Bonney watched him move slowly and carefully as he entered the bus. The driver said, "Take your time, Pop, no sense in hurrying."

The people in the front of the bus all seemed mesmerized by Pop as he placed his coins in the box, paused, pointed at the driver, and then said, looking directly at Bonney, "I'm such a lucky man. People are always kind to me. Do you know why I am walking like this? I was hit by a car. My hip was broken, but everyone around was so kind to me. They helped me. I'm so blessed - people *like* me."

Pop smiled directly at Bonney and she smiled back at him. She felt her heart relax. A wave of peace passed through her. Tears flooding her eyes, Bonney wondered, "Is this really happening? Does he know what I'm going through?...He seems to know."

The elderly man with the cane healed her in that moment of service with his words and smile and warmth. Bonney's mind flashed to the hospital patients and wished that this same loving force could find its way onto the hospital unit that night.

Case Study: Pietro

We recall another powerful example of service, and how it inspired us, when we visited a retreat center in Tuscany. With a dear Florentine friend, we drove deep into the countryside to find a Franciscan monastery that was now being used for drug rehabilitation. After a main highway and three country roads, we found a little sign pointing to a steep lane that led up to the center.

A young man named Pietro greeted us at the outer gate and took us on a pre-arranged tour. He had a handsome, almost beautiful face, and a sweetness to his manner. Later, he told us that he reserves 20 minute for a tour and was surprised that we had ended up talking together for five hours. These things can happen when you're standing together in a 13th Century grotto in which St. Francis of Assisi taught his followers: you just go outside of time.

The jasmine and rose vines were heavy with flowers covering the ancient walls of the monastery and giving off the sweetest fragrances. The cloudy June day shifted to bright sun causing plays of light in the trees and onto the golden travertine of the cloister walls as Pietro told us about the development of the center.

In the 1960s, a visionary monk was looking for a place to hold retreats. The monk was reacting to a trend he was observing - many people seemed directionless, lost, in crisis, and doubting themselves in some fundamental way. The monk was given permission to take over an abandoned Franciscan monastery for his work. He envisioned it as a place where people could reflect and reconnect with their values. In our words, he wanted to help them to gain access to their guiding inner wisdom and realize their life purpose.

The abandoned monastery had over the years become a physical disaster. Walls had collapsed, garbage was everywhere, all the windows were broken. The monk, raised in the countryside and used to hard work, took on the repair work with some of the local people volunteering to help him.

Then, as Pietro put it, "the drug boom hit Italy." Heroin had arrived big-time. Suddenly, there was a wave of people in trouble. The monk's retreat center began to be thought of as one possible answer. The monk took people in as residents and put them to work repairing the monastery. Grateful families began to make financial contributions. The monk never charged any fee, and contributions alone kept the retreat center going.

The monk personally wasn't the slightest bit interested in drug treatment. Instead, he was interested in "the seed," the higher potential in each person. He therefore gave the residents a chance to work at different tasks in order to create the conditions for their seed, their potential, to reveal itself to them. You can surely hear our view of dormant transpersonal resources in the monk's ideas.

Pietro said he had found his seed by communicating honestly with people. He was listening very closely one day to what someone was telling him, and he felt the desire to speak back kindly but with absolute honesty. He could feel the relief of honest words coming out of his mouth. This simple act put him into a state of peace and comfort inside his own skin, a feeling he hadn't had since he was a little child. He began to seek out more situations in which communication was the task, such as accompanying the monk to meetings with the local townspeople or helping out with tours of the center.

He began to apply this mindful listening to all interactions. He would center himself so that he could both listen carefully and be aware of what he wanted to honestly say in return. We could palpably feel the results of his practice. He had a quiet presence that made us want to tell him our intimate thoughts. His peace and his focus seemed to be totally for us, as if he was speaking directly to some longing deep inside us.

After we left Pietro and got back on the country roads toward the highway, we were filled with sadness. It seemed to be an odd emotion, since the visit had been so inspiring. We pulled off the road into dark woods and kept talking until we could understand the sadness. We felt that a deeper part of us, inspired by Pietro's words and the monk's accomplishments, had been activated, and it was now causing us to review our life and question our real worth. Our longing to truly know our life purpose had been fully awakened by Pietro.

But what was our seed? What had we, if anything, done with it? Pietro had been like a mirror held up to our own path of service, challenging us to reconnect with what truly mattered to us.

The Path of Social Action and Justice

If I am not for myself, who will be for me? If I am

only for myself, what am I? And, if not now, when?

—HILLEL

An extension of the path of service is social action. You may think that political activism is about as far away from the transpersonal as you can get, but in fact it combines two aspects of the transpersonal path: liberation from an absorption in your own habitual personality patterns; the conscious choice to unify with the experience of others.

Courageous leaders such as Gandhi and Martin Luther King clearly pointed to their own transpersonal nature as they pursued justice for others.

Gandhi said, "Fearlessness is the first requisite of spirituality." Martin Luther King, in a sermon he gave in 1967, less than four months before his assassination, spoke of touching a higher love where "...you love all men, not because you like them, not because their ways appeal to you, but you love them because God loves them."

Case Study: Annemarie

We've had several clients over the years who thought their social activism was the opposite of spirituality. One of them, Annemarie, equated her activism with being realistic and practical. She viewed spirituality as the exact opposite - a kind of useless, passive fantasy. She described herself as disgusted by religious or spiritual leaders who would comment on social issues but do nothing about them.

She had grown up in a rural Midwestern town. She always felt drawn to the Native American culture that existed around her. While in high school in the early 1970s, she began getting involved in the Native American rights movement. Eventually, she worked with the tribal councils on issues related to land rights.

This was a time in Annemarie's life when she felt exhilarated by the work she was doing. She experienced deep satisfaction and felt enriched by the friendships she made within the Native American community.

Twenty-five years later, Annemarie was living in New York City and working as a psychiatric social worker. She had reached a level of discouragement and compassion fatigue and sought help through counseling. She had achieved success in her career and personal life, but she was exhausted by the unmet needs of the people she worked with. She was clearly in need of an opening to the transpersonal aspect of her nature.

Her identity as a political activist had been with her from those early days in the Native American movement to her current job in social work. In exploring Annemarie's activism, she was encouraged to wonder about the motivation and intention in her choices. What difference did it make to Annemarie if Native Americans kept their rights to tribal lands? Why was she willing to work long hours in a New York City battered women's shelter? What is at the heart of the person motivated by altruism and social concerns?

In response to these questions, Annemarie used words like "justice" and "empowerment" to explain her actions. Why was justice important to her? She was not an oppressed or battered person. Like many other people, she could choose to "look the other way" and deny these realities.

What began to emerge was Annemarie's deep feelings of oneness with people. She spoke of the pain she experienced when she watched the news on television or heard of injustices or suffering. In such moments, she experienced herself as transcending her own separateness and instead feeling at one with everyone. It could well be that, in one of her moments of unity through service, she was awakening that same region of the brain that Newberg and D'Aquila identified as *absolute unitary being*.

Reassessing her work in the light of these feelings, she began to see her activism as a transpersonal path. This was an exciting shift for Annemarie. She had always thought spirituality would not be available to her. She had thought her outrage at suffering in the world would keep her from the promises of spirituality as sources of peace and wisdom. Instead, she now saw that her activism was her transpersonal practice.

The Path of Meditation

The Ultimate Truth is wordless,

the silence within the silence.

More than the absence of speech,

more than the absence of words,

Ultimate Truth is the seamless being-in-place

that comes with attending to Reality.

—*SHIMON BEN GAMLIEL*

As we've described earlier, all of our **Huntington Method** practices involve entering an inward, meditative state. When you meditate, you are directing your awareness in a new way. Rather than your mind wandering all over the place, from one thought to another, to a feeling, a sensation, an urge, you are choosing instead to focus your awareness on one object. As you do this, you will tend to have one of three experiences:

- Despite your intention to meditate, you will get lost in the wanderings of your mental activity;
- You will go into a trance, space out, and not know where your mind went;

- You will stay present. When you stay present, you are opening the way to the transpersonal aspect of your nature.

The practice of staying present gives you immediate benefits. You will be able to focus on any activity more easily, and you will feel increasing periods of deep physical relaxation. As you continue, new experiences will become more common, including dynamic stillness, inner peace, light pervading joy, and intuitive visions and ideas.

What is happening is that your awareness is being temporarily freed from the heaviness and constriction of your habitual patterns, and you are discovering a part of you that is already light and harmonious. You are not creating this harmonious state by meditating, but rather you are discovering it through meditation. You are discovering that awareness itself is naturally serene. Assagioli described this quality of your awareness as "something sure, permanent, and indestructible."

Case Study: John

After his first heart attack, John, a 58 year old teacher, began to look for treatment of his coronary artery disease. He decided to try the approach of cardiologist Dean Ornish. Ornish's patients have been able to reverse coronary arterial clogging, to reduce or discontinue medication, to reduce or end chest pain, to lose weight while eating more, and to feel more energetic and calm (Ornish, 1990).

All of this is accomplished without surgery or medication. It is accomplished through the alternative health practices of stress management (meditation, imagery, hatha yoga), diet, exercise, stopping smoking and other addictions, and group support.

After trying the Ornish approach for a week, John gave up. He could not comply with all the lifestyle changes. In frustration, he called Ornish on the telephone and asked him to recommend only the single most important practice in the approach. Dr. Ornish immediately told John, "Meditate."

John was surprised. He thought surely that diet or exercise would be the priority. John asked Ornish why meditation was the key practice. In response, he was told that meditation counteracts "the pounding your body takes from your worried mind."

Discussion. The worry pattern draws your intelligence and your imagination into its service and produces a fearful version of reality. Oddly, worry is often treated as if it is helpful. It appears to be watching out for you. By worrying, you even get the feeling you are doing something about a situation, as if worry was somehow capable of changing reality. In **Part Five: Summary of the Huntington Method,** we discuss worry as a function of the fear center of the brain and how it is treated on the path of transpersonal development.

Types of Meditation

Physical benefits through meditation have been well documented for many years (see, for example, Greeson, 2008). Mental and emotional benefits are subtler and are therefore more difficult to measure. Stress reduction is the most researched variable of meditation because it can be operationalized and quantified through medical technology. Kabat-Zinn (1991) called his initial hospital-based meditation training program a *stress reduction* clinic. Since its start in one hospital, the use of meditation as a healthcare intervention has grown internationally (Fjorback & Walach, 2012).

In general, meditation practices can be classified as concentrative, receptive, and creative. All meditative traditions have all three types of meditation, but tend to emphasize one practice over another, especially for beginning students.

Concentrative meditation. Concentrative practices emphasize a single-minded focus on one object - the breath, a phrase, a thought, an image, a repeated movement. In such practices, the goal is for you to ignore all other experiences and to keep returning attention to the single meditative object.

This concentrated focus on one object has great potential: it can lead to states of blissful ease. Such experiences can give you an ability to change your state from fear to peace and thus give you a new sense of self-control.

Examples of concentrative practices include:

- the focus on breath in the early phases of Zen and mind-fulness training
- focus on mantra in transcendental meditation
- focus on a single word linked with the breath cycle (the relaxation response practice) developed by cardiologist Herbert Benson.

A concentrative focus on breath is particularly effective. This is true because difficult moments of fear and anxiety produce holding of breath or shortening of breath, resulting in at least mild hyperventilating. Hyperventilating in turn produces more excitation, more anxiety. Focus on the breath restores a more normal breathing cycle, and the change in respiration rate calms the entire physical self. Having developed a concentrative meditative practice, several of our clients can now manage situations that were previously sources of phobic fear.

As effective as they are, concentrative meditation practices also have limitations. By turning attention over and over again to one object, all other experiences are ignored. For example, your inner wisdom may be opening to you through words or images or feelings, but the concentrative practice counsels you to pay no attention to such experiences. In the extreme, experiences may be repressed, kept out of consciousness. Concentrative meditation can bring profound relaxation to your mind and body, but its ignoring of thoughts and feelings may slow down new learning and transpersonal development.

Receptive meditation. Receptive practices begin with a concentration practice, such as focus on breathing. They then gradually let awareness open to the stream of experiences: body sensations, thoughts, feelings, moods, sounds, energy shifts. Our **Huntington Method** practices, **Stream of Consciousness** and **Centering and Naming,** are two examples of receptive meditation.

Case Study: Glen

Glen, a 35 year old with a diagnosis of HIV positive was referred by a physician because of episodes of extreme fear and anger. Glen had refused medication for his episodes, rightly asserting he was having extreme feelings because of the extreme situation he was in. He said he did not want to learn any mental tricks or simple relaxation practices or be hypnotized out of his fear and anger. He was sure about what he didn't want, but he did need some new way to cope with his suffering.

He was first trained in the **Stream of Consciousness (Practice 4)**. After two periods of three minutes each working with the practice, he was then instructed to

(1) consider his breath as his center

(2) to be interested in whatever thought or image or feeling or sensation pulled him away from his breath, away from his center

---

(3) to keep his attention long enough on the off-center experience to know what it was, e.g., worrying

(4) to mentally note, "Worry"

(5) to then return his attention to his breath, to his center.

This **Centering and Naming** practice (**Practice 5**) of movement from center to off-center and back to center was characterized as the normal flow of the meditation period. No attempt was made, as it is in concentrative meditation, to stay fixedly focused on the center. Rather, the receptive practice is to be able to receive whatever is being experienced, and then to be able to center oneself again.

His request to not deny his feelings was being honored, and at the same time he was learning how to be with them in a new way. Recent brain research (Hoelzel et al., 2011) demonstrates that this awareness practice strengthens important integrative fibers in the brain that modify fear.

Within two weeks of daily practice of **Centering and Naming**, Glen began to realize he was having a wide variety of internal experiences, of which fear and anger were only two. When the fear or anger did come, they were like big waves, taking him over. But then they would pass. He began to realize fear and anger were present along with questioning, sensitivity, religious searching, self-hatred, self-compassion, practical thinking, remembering, and so on. His fear and anger were not blunted or denied but were instead experienced, in a receptive way, within a larger array of experience. This practice has been successfully taught to many medical patients in extreme situations (Kabat-Zinn, 1991).

Glen was learning that he could identify with the fearful and angry thoughts and feelings - or just notice them and let them pass. He was learning that he had a choice.

Creative meditation. Creative meditation can be added to concentrative and receptive practices. Creative meditation brings the vast resource of the imagination into meditative practice.

The absence of the imagination in many meditative practices is an unnecessary deprivation. The imagination is a dominant force in human nature and holds great potential in promoting well-being.

Two religious traditions that greatly utilize the imagination in the path of meditation are Roman Catholicism and Tibetan Buddhism. They both utilize art and images to awaken transpersonal qualities. The imagination is also central to the meditation practices of the two pioneers of the transpersonal path, Carl Jung and Roberto Assagioli. Creative meditation is the most complex form of meditation because of the interaction between the conscious mind, imagination, feeling states, and periods of emptiness and silence.

Case Study: Frances

Frances, 50 years old, was terminally ill with lung cancer. She presented the belief that she had somehow caused herself to have this fatal disease. This belief turned out to be part of a dominant personality pattern in which she blamed herself and criticized herself for anything that goes wrong. Richard did not accept such a belief, but also had to respect Frances's way of understanding her suffering. Frances asked for help in coming to terms with her situation.

She was guided to follow her breathing in her belly (**Centering, Practice 3**), then to open to her stream of experiences (**Stream of Consciousness, Practice 4**), and then to imagine a wisdom figure with whom she could dialogue in her mind (**Inner Wisdom, Practice 8).** It was then suggested that she ask the wisdom figure about the illness.

In her imagination, Frances met a spiritual teacher who brought her to a scene from early childhood. In the memory, she is locked out of her house and desperately has to urinate. The child urinates in her pants and then hides in the backyard in humiliation.

At the conscious level, this disturbing memory seemed to Frances to have nothing to do with her question about her illness. She returned to her creative meditative practice and asked the imagined spiritual teacher for more information. She was led to another disturbing childhood memory.

Frances began to realize these images were showing her how many times she wanted to die from humiliation. She then felt compassion for the little girl in the memories and cried with relief at feeling kindness toward herself. Her self-hatred softened as she continued her meditation practice. Her dying process was approached with greater peace of mind.

The Path of Physical Training and the Senses

Melanie described why she loved skiing so much. She would find herself on a steep, quiet slope where she could not see all the way down the mountain. Everything around her would appear totally white as sunlight glistened on the surface of the snow. Completely at one with her skis, her body supple and balanced, speeding into timelessness, at one with the mountain, no thoughts, no more Melanie, just the moment – that was all she ever wanted. The longing for those moments always brought tears to her eyes.

The path of the senses is a way to transpersonal experience which emphasizes the body. Physical activities such as Melanie's can create the feeling of oneness, of being part of something greater. Athletes know this moment when they let go of trying to force their efforts. It is an experience of flow, of effortless effort. It occurs when the basketball player cannot miss the shot. He is described as "in the zone." The ball goes in every time. It is no longer about winning the game.

It is an awareness state in which the player is at one with the object of the action. The other players can see it when it is happening.

There are different ways to experience oneness through the body and the senses. The experience of learning to use your body in a new way, of mastering a skill to the point of not having to struggle to do it, can create this experience.

Hatha yoga, QiGong, Tai Chi, Reiki, and certain forms of martial arts training are examples of the path of the senses, the path of the body. These practices connect you with the life energy we are all participating in. In the yogic tradition, this life energy is called prana. In Taoism, it is called chi or Qi. Both systems are referring to the life energy which exists within us but is at the same time connected to and flowing from universal life energy, the vitalizing force of all living beings.

Healing energy. In western cultures, this interaction of personal and universal energy has been called magnetism, libido, bioenergy, subtle energy. In more religious terms, it is spoken of as the holy spirit. Practitioners of acupuncture, therapeutic touch, Reiki, healing touch, craniosacral therapy and other forms of body healing utilize this energy in healthcare settings, as do ministers and other faith healers in religious settings.

Pioneering researchers such as Elmer Green have studied energy healers to measure changes in electro-magnetic fields caused by their practices (DiCarlo, 1996). Preliminary results indicated that practitioners do have the ability to affect physical systems at the level of electro-magnetism. This research is an example of the new synthesis of science and spiritual traditions (Schaub, 1995; NCCAM, 2011). For some scientifically-minded health professionals, including ourselves, this study of universal energy can become a spiritual practice and a source of transpersonal experiences.

The Path of Ceremony and Ritual

...They went down to the River and Made a Sweat Lodge. As before, the Stones were Heated, and The Songs Sung. But this time they were sung by All the People, because they All Knew them. And they Held their Braids to their Heads and Listened to their Hearts, and to those of their Brothers and Sisters, and they were Healed. —HYEMEYOHSTS STORM

Case Study: Mary

Mary joined a local 12 Step Al-Anon meeting for partners of people in recovery from alcoholism. It was available everyday at noon, and she went as many days as she could. It provided her with a brief sanctuary from the hectic work day and gave her a place to express herself honestly without fear of judgment.

The format of the meeting was the same each time. Each person spoke only if they chose to. No one commented directly on what was said, but someone might comment on how they identified with the feelings. At the end of the meeting, a brief prayer was said.

This ceremony has been a part of Mary's life for the past four years, ever since her husband entered AA. During his active alcoholism, she had completely lost touch with her feelings. The Al-Anon meeting became a ceremony for contacting and expressing feelings.

Discussion. The path of ceremony and ritual uses communal and individual rituals and symbolic actions to deepen a sense of oneness. Part of the richness of these practices come from the powerful synergy of a like-minded group of people joining together with shared intention. This act of communion and community has the ability to draw people out beyond their separateness and into a connection with something greater. For Mary and many other people, their participation in 12 Step meetings serves this purpose. There is tremendous healing in knowing "I am not alone."

Formal ceremonies. In more formalized ceremonies, the setting, structure and incorporated elements - special garments, candles, incense, prayers, music, and symbolic objects - create a sacred space that serves as an invitation to let go of your habitual self. Pageantry, theater, and dance are creative expressions that are often incorporated into ceremonies. Part of the intention is to allow the individual observers to become participants in the sacred story being told through the symbolic actions.

The Path of Knowledge

The sense of wonder is based on the admission that our intellect is a limited and finite instrument of information and expression, reserved for specific practical uses, but not fit to represent the completeness of our being...It is here that we come in direct touch with a reality which may baffle our intellect but which fills us with that sense of wonder which opens the way to the inner sanctuary of the mind, to the heart of the great mystery of life and death... —LAMA GOVINDA

Case Study: Veronica

As part of her recovery from alcoholism, Veronica reads the Bible everyday. She takes a few words and meditates on them.

She had lost interest in religion in adolescence, seeing churchgoers as hypocrites who did not live the principles of their religion. Now, drug-free and struggling with vulnerability, Veronica knew she needed to help herself. She went briefly to AA but did not like the way the men behaved toward her. She knew her judgment was off and knew she'd probably pick the wrong man to get involved with. She joined a women's counseling group and was impressed by one of the group members who had returned to her traditional religious roots.

Veronica bought a Bible and began studying on her own. Then one day she casually overheard somehow say that the Bible is really a way to study how the world works. She suddenly felt free of her resistance against her early religious experiences, and she saw the Bible as a book of knowledge. She found that some of the teaching stories would start to make her cry, as if something was opening and releasing inside her. She'd then feel lighter and calmer throughout the day.

Veronica can be seen as having entered the path of knowledge and wisdom. This path is the mental search for what is true. The search can take very different forms and come from many different perspectives.

The search for truth. You may think of scientists and researchers as people who are pre-eminently rational and dismiss spirituality as unreal. Seemingly ephemeral subjects such as consciousness need to be reduced to measurable and mechanical terms in order to be taken seriously. A current example of this is in comparing human consciousness to computer functions.

But what was the origin of the scientific method? It was Francis Bacon in the 16th Century trying to bring the search for universal truth into the natural world. Up until that time, the university was the province of the aristocracy and the clergy who believed that truth and ultimate knowledge could be found through rhetoric and discourse.

Pioneering thinkers such as Bacon, by contrast, sought truth by observing natural phenomena in the minutest detail, methodically, conscientiously, and objectively free of the constraints of theology and politics. The search for truth was now available to the common man, not just the nobles and clergy.

What is it that drives the scientist to know more and more, to always have another question? She is on a quest. What is it that moves the mathematician and physicist? Is it a sense of awe at the complexity of things? Every answer brings new questions. Knowledge expands out farther and farther, to the infinity of the universe, and deeper and deeper down to smaller and smaller particles.

Wilder Penfield was a mid-20th Century Toronto neurosurgeon and a pioneer in brain research. Toward the end of his career, he wrote *The Mystery of the Mind* (1975). The book was a personal account of his years of study in which he beautifully articulated the path of knowledge.

His lifelong search had been to understand the nature of consciousness as it related to the physical organ of the brain. He wanted to understand if neuro-electric and chemical reactions could explain the existence of awareness in the human experience. He came to following conclusion:

> "...the nature of the mind remains, still, a mystery that science has not solved. But it is, I believe, a mystery that science will solve someday. In that day of understanding, I predict that true prophets will rejoice, for they will discover in the scientist a long-awaited ally in the search for Truth" (1975, p. xiii).

An interesting postscript on Penfield's work happened to us at a medical conference. We met the nurse who had assisted him in his research. As we got to talking, she said, "He didn't want to tell anyone, but he was really looking for the soul."

This search for truth is certainly exemplified in the research-er or scientist, but it can also be seen in Veronica who made commitment to her own study of truth. The potential of such study is exemplified in the Zen phrase:

> "To study the Way is to study the self.
> To study the self is to forget the self.
> To forget the self is to be enlightened
> by all the things of the universe."

The Path of Devotion and Prayer

I am so small I can barely be seen. How can this great love be inside me? —RUMI

The path of devotion and prayer is characterized by surrender, adoration, and worship. It is the primary path of any religious tradition in which belief and faith are emphasized. Its premise is that we are too small to know the ultimate answers, but that we can enjoy, even love, the wonders we are part of. Far from the researcher who personally seeks out knowledge, this path asks you to give up the search for knowledge and to give in, to surrender to powers greater than you. This concept of surrender is not a matter of resignation but rather an empowered awareness that something greater than your separate self is involved in your life and that you need to open to this universal aspect of reality.

Dr. Larry Dossey, one of the pioneers of integrative medicine, studied and synthesized experimental research in prayer (1994). His thoughts on the nature of prayer are provocative and offer new possibilities for the devotional path:

> "The prevailing notion that prayer is asking for something is woefully incomplete. I want to get away from that common way of looking at prayer. Prayer for me is any psychological act which brings us closer to the transcendent. Prayer may involve words. It can involve silence, nonactivity. It can even be done in the subconscious or when we sleep at night. So I prefer the use the term 'prayerfulness' to capture those activities we have traditionally called prayer."

Case Study: George

By the age of six, it was obvious George was different. He did not play the way boys usually do. It had nothing to do with his mind. He was clearly highly intelligent and sensitive and loving. His father, an active alcoholic, did not like this difference in George. The father taunted George, and George's brother learned to join in with the father in his taunts. His mother did not help George either. Afraid of the father's rages, she began to beat George whenever she saw behaviors she felt were unacceptable to the father.

What can any child make of this insanity? The young mind has no perspective on such abuse. The child completely assumes it is his fault. To the child, it is clear there is something very wrong with him.

From this history, we can assume George lived in a constant state of fear. He vividly remembers a scene from the third grade. The teacher raised her hand to adjust her glasses, and George literally jumped out of his chair: he was sure he was going to be hit.

By thirteen, George knew what was different about him. He was developing secret crushes on boys in his class. His sexuality did not have a name yet, but his classmates had started to call him a sissy. Between home and school, George had no relief from fear and humiliation. His only escape was in the local Catholic church. He would go into the church and pray in front of a statue of the Virgin Mary.

George's prayers in front of the Mary statue brought him some peace. He would feel that someone in the world - Mary - was caring for him. He felt devoted to her and felt she knew his suffering. When he would be in a humiliating or frightening moment at school, he would think of Mary, and some calm would come to him. Feeling that no one else in the world was on his side, he felt Mary was with him.

At the same time, George was searching for anything else that would ease his emotional pain. George first found it in alcohol and then in tranquilizers and sedatives. He got the alcohol from his father's supply and the pills from his mother's supply. The entire family was medicating their emotional pain.

George also got to know the drug dealers at school for a second source of pills. He eventually developed a third source of pills: doctors. By the end of high school, he was able to convince any doctor of his need for a prescription for tranquilizers. By the time he went away to college, he knew he was gay and he knew he could not live without pills and alcohol.

George entered recovery at the age of 31. He had lost his second job because of verbal fights with his co-workers. The rage that is the legacy of some abused children had been coming out of him more and more. The drugs were no longer giving him relief. By now in his addiction, he was taking drugs to offset the feelings from taking drugs. The original emotional pain was now long buried inside the addiction.

When George lost his second job, he was broke and soon lost his apartment. He had no choice: go back to his family house or live on the street. His father had died two years ago. His brother was married, lived far away and was reported to be an active alcoholic. His mother lived in the family home by herself.

George moved into the family house completely despondent. He was hitting bottom. He went to a local AA meeting but felt afraid of disclosing anything personal in the town he had grown up in. He began to go to meetings in a nearby city.

George had an immediately positive reaction to the religious language of AA. He began returning to church and tried to pray to Mary again. Thinking he was by now a sophisticated and cynical adult, he thought that the praying would feel foolish and childish. Instead, he found it powerful and helpful. His devotion to Mary was bringing him a much-needed depth of peace far beyond relaxation.

Discussion. What actually happens to someone in a state of devotion? In George's mind, he is deliberately turning his awareness away from fear as he begins to imagine Mary's face. He thinks about who she is. He begins to feel the pain she must have felt at the death of her son, Jesus, and he senses she would understand his pain. He is both contemplating Mary as an empathic mother, and he is also turning his own empathy toward Mary. He is identifying with her. He is going beyond his personality and awakening a loving oneness inside himself. In doing so, he begins to feel those most resilient qualities that come from our transpersonal nature – hope and inspiration.

PART FOUR:

Obstacles to the Transpersonal

Repression of the Sublime

We said earlier that transpersonal practices have emerged from spiritual traditions, and so it understandable that they are associated with each other. One negative result of this association is that clients who have obstacles to religion and spirituality will often have obstacles to transpersonal work. Suggesting that there is anything beyond the self they know evokes in them a cynicism, a cringe, a knee-jerk rejection. The transpersonal aspect of their nature, objectively real and beneficial, gets lumped in with everything else that suggests to them religious and spiritual fantasies.

Assagioli referred to this rejecting attitude as the "repression of the sublime" (1965). The repression is the denial, neglect, or dismissal of the transpersonal. If you recall the story of the business executive who went into a state of blissful oneness in his backyard, it took him three years to talk to anyone about his experience after his wife had dismissed it as weird.

The *blissful oneness* of our executive, *connected and in love with everything*, is not your typical night in suburbia. He had spontaneously discovered what the mystics and saints of every time and culture have told us is our fundamental nature. The universe is comprised of energy, they say, and we are immersed in it and ceaselessly participating in its pervading unifying oneness. Whenever our awareness is temporarily liberated from our focus on our individual self, we may get a glimpse of the vast, non-visible world we are part of.

In a way, the goal of transpersonal development could be distilled down to helping to lift the repression of the sublime in your own nature. To do this, you need to consider the classic obstacles that could prevent this goal from happening.

Five Types of Obstacles

There are five general types of obstacles that can block transpersonal discovery (Schaub & Follman, 1996):

- childhood experiences with religion
- traumas that destroyed trust
- social fears
- ego fears
- irrational thinking.

Your work in transpersonal development calls upon you to be an intelligent role model for your clients and to normalize the transpersonal as a natural part of everyone. You can do this most effectively by gaining self-knowledge of any of your own obstacles to your transpersonal nature. We all have some variation of them.

Obstacles Originating in Childhood Experiences with Religion

Childhood training leading to immature spirituality. This first obstacle is rooted in childhood religious training about God as the father in the sky looking down on the earth. For children with this training, it is natural to pray to the God in the sky for help.

The child, however, does not see an outcome to the prayer. Praying that his parents would not get divorced, the parents get divorced anyway. Praying that the dead pet would be revived back to life, the pet is buried and gone forever. Praying that the other children at school will stop taunting him, the taunts go on.

The child's mind has not yet developed the capacity to tolerate ambiguity. The child's thinking is black or white, always or never, yes or no. The child prays for something specific, and the absence of help from God disappoints the child deeply.

The disappointment doesn't go away. A woman recently discharged from the hospital after treatment for lymphoma asked Bonney for help in learning meditation to reduce anxiety. In the course of the interview, she described an angry meeting with a hospital chaplain who had advised her to look to God for help. When asked what had angered her about the chaplain, she sneered and said, "There's no guy in the sky looking out for me - that's all lies." Her childhood disappointment was still very present in her 55 year old face.

This obstacle of disappointment is not only present in individuals. As one example, Christianity has declined dramatically in Europe every since World War Two (1939-1945). The war deaths of over forty million people ended the belief in a protective God.

Negative childhood experiences with organized religion. These negative experiences include:

- seeing hypocrisy in adult religious leaders
- feeling insulted or humiliated at religious meetings
- being frightened by religious dogmas of punishment
- witnessing family conflict over religion.

The result of these negative experiences is that the client is always in conflict trying to reconcile the negative vs. positive aspects of his religious upbringing. Transpersonal possibilities get lost in the inner conflict.

The negative experiences can be severe. Direct physical abuse and sexual abuse by religious workers destroys a child's ability to ever find peace or comfort from his religion. It often creates a lifelong mistrust of any formal religious structure.

Another negative experience with religion is the idea of God as a father figure. The clear male model of God in some religions can be troubling if the children's own father was frightening. This can be compounded, as referred to earlier, if the male God does not intervene on the child's behalf.

God as male has contributed to the exclusion of women from full participation in many religious systems. Reaction against this exclusion has resulted in growing interest in Goddess traditions, nature focused practices, or neutral (e.g., the universe) non-religious terminology. These explorations are motivated by the desire to go beyond cultural-bound descriptions of God as male.

No experiences with religion. Some children are never exposed to a model of spirituality or philosophical thought. Others are raised in an environment of overt hostility to religion and spirituality. Unless an interest develops later, the child can become an adult who simply accepts society's reality as all there is. Society's goals become his goals, and he focuses only on the problems society presents to him. Anything transpersonal is considered to be unreal.

Obstacles Originating in Traumas that Destroyed Trust

Trauma destroys trust in the world as a place of order and safety. Examples of trauma include physical violence, rape, incest, sexual molestation, emotional abuse, death of parent or close family member or friend, abandonment, serious illnesses, hospitalizations and surgical procedures, civil unrest, violent neighborhoods, destructive storms, harassment and terror.

Such experiences reorganize your mind and your nervous system around fear and vigilance. Until you can move toward healing, you will be living in fight/flight/freeze reactivity as an ongoing experience (McFarlane, 2010). Access to inner peace will be difficult because it asks you to relax your habitual and protective vigilant state.

Obstacles Originating In Social Fears

Think again of our business executive in his suburban backyard. Why didn't he talk to anyone about his profound discovery of oneness? He told his wife about the energy flowing through him, she called it *weird*, and he went into silence about it for three years.

As we said earlier, transpersonal experience is a subject often treated with ignorance and repression. Though a totally natural part of human nature, people speak hesitatingly, guardedly, about their transpersonal experiences, as if they were discussing a taboo subject in public. Fears of social disapproval include fears of criticism, embarrassment, exclusion, ridicule, being seen as odd, being seen as grandiose.

Obstacles Originating in Ego Fears

Your ego is an organizing process oriented toward biological survival and social approval. When the ego is confronted with an unexplainable experience from the transpersonal level of your nature, its initial reaction is often to deprive the experience of any meaning. Our business executive's wife was frightened by her husband's experience and immediately denied its importance.

Through this denial, your ego minimizes anxiety. Denial of unexplainable experiences retains the illusion that everything is known and in your control. This is understandable because the illusion of control has an important developmental function. It allows you to risk the many uncertainties of life without being stopped by too much anxiety or too much depression. How many situations could you tolerate if you realized how little control you have over life? Without your control illusion, could you tolerate the fact that we are all traveling together on a spinning planet moving through infinite space?

But under extreme circumstances, your ego can't retain the illusion of control. Such circumstances include impending violence, destructive and manipulative relationships, a betrayal of trust, serious illness, severe economic changes, drug addiction, physical entrapment, natural disasters. The illusion of personal control collapses, and the result can be a massive surge of anxiety (a panic attack). In many cases, a second panic attack is never experienced, but the one episode of panic can create a haunting fear of a recurrence.

Your ego therefore has an inherent problem with your transpersonal nature. The transpersonal dimension is largely unknown and unfamiliar to you, and you don't know how it might alter you.

The ego exists for functional purposes and is not the enemy of transpersonal/spiritual development. If you are reading any spiritual book that tells you to get rid of your ego, we advise you to get rid of the book.

Many spiritual traditions recognize the problem of the ego's control needs and often counsel that the ego is an obstacle to spiritual development. Some traditions even suggest the ego is an enemy. This is an unnatural and harmful view. The ego exists for functional purposes and is not the enemy of transpersonal/spiritual development. If you are reading any spiritual book that tells you to get rid of your ego, we advise you to get rid of the book. As Assagioli put it, "The ego is a personal reflection of higher organizing processes in nature, and so the idea of getting rid of the ego is silly" (undated notes).

Ego fears about transpersonal experiences are expressed in the following ways:

- fear of "going out there" and never coming back
- fear of going crazy
- fear of getting "high" through spirituality

- fear of becoming dysfunctional
- fear of being changed in some unknown way
- fear of becoming indifferent to everyday life
- fear of becoming God-like and grandiose.

Transpersonal experiences, in fact, prove to be beneficial to the ego. They help your fear-based, survival-based sense of self to calm down. Once you have realized this benefit, you can align your ego with the desire for more transpersonal discoveries.

There is nevertheless some merit in these ego fears. It is when transpersonal work is done in an unethical way.

We have seen ungrounded transpersonal/spiritual practices that can lead to physical and mental imbalance and harm. Known in our community as psychotherapists trained in meditation and open to spirituality, we frequently were referred people who had just left cult-like spiritual groups. Filled with anxiety and self-doubt, they needed to recover their healthy ego and personal dignity.

While the majority of spiritual teachers we have met are dedicated and caring, the psychological naïveté, poor judgment, and even abuses of some gurus and/or spiritual masters are an established fact. This harmful behavior is aided by students who refuse to think for themselves, ignore their gut instincts, and blindly follow bad advice. We have been relieved to see that over the years more and more health professionals, working under the responsibility of licenses and ethical guidelines, have begun to do transpersonal work. This gives clients an alternative way to proceed with their transpersonal/spiritual development.

Obstacles Originating In Irrational Thinking

Predictable irrational thoughts regarding the transpersonal include:

- it is escapism and fantasy
- it has nothing to do with this world
- it is childish and regressive
- it is not scientific
- it is strange to be interested in such things
- only special people know about it
- if you are spiritual, you never get angry
- if you are spiritual, nothing bothers you
- you become indifferent to the world
- it is irrational.

While you could choose to investigate these possible obstacles with your client, it is more effective to offer your client a direct experience first. Experience is the best teacher. We'd suggest starting with the early **Inner Peace** practices

(**Practices 1 – 5**). They all produce a relaxation and, in some cases, a relaxation more profound than the client has ever felt before. As a convincing first experience, relaxation works. It is its own benefit, and it points the way to more experiences waiting in your client's transpersonal nature.

If the client finds it difficult to let go into the experience, the first obstacle has already revealed itself. There is something in the possibility of deep relaxation that concerns the client. The exploration of the obstacle then becomes a collaborative dialogue between the two of you.

PART FIVE:

A Summary of The Huntington Method

"What you are looking for is what is looking."

—*ST. FRANCIS OF ASSISI*

There are three general phases of transpersonal development:

- Moving from fear to choice
- The opening of the personality
- Moving from separateness to oneness

They each represent a new development in your relationship to your transpersonal nature.

Moving from Fear to Choice

1. Research indicates that your brain has a region - a fear center - which scans the environment for signs of danger (Shin & Liberzon, 2010). The *environment* you scan includes both a) the *outside world* of people and events, and b) the *inside world* of your own mind and body.

2. This scanning is your brain in a vigilant state. It is a reflection of the brain/mind's instinct for survival. The normal brain is biased in favor of paying attention to anything negative in order to survive (Hanson, 2009).

3. Your survival instinct motivates you to want to control life. Your fear center scans for any possible threat so that the threat can be controlled.

4. Threat exists, and paying attention to it is essential at times. Problems develop when you become attached to

being vigilant as a habitual way of living. Being primed for danger can become your default setting. Your awareness can become the servant of your fears (Follman, 2012).

5. When your fear center perceives threat, real or imagined, it sends a) worries and warnings into your mind, and b) anxiety into your body. These are alarm signals.

6. Worries, warnings and anxiety are compelling. They grab your attention. If you had the luxury of examining the factual truth of the alarm signals, you'd find that most perceived threats are exaggerated or even imagined by your fear center.

    However, you usually don't have the luxury of examining an alarm signal. Worries, warnings and anxiety quickly stimulate your protective instincts: fight, flight or freeze.

7. The fight reaction is an attempt to exert power over fear-based feelings. It is an act of *willfulness,* a summoning of your life energy to impose your willpower over a situation in which you feel vulnerable.

    The flight/freeze reaction is an attempt to escape, to withdraw your life energy from a vulnerable situation. In contrast to willfulness, escape and withdrawal is an act of *will-lessness.*

8. Willful and will-less reactions show up in your mind, feelings, body, and spirit (Schaub & Schaub, 1997). The list, below, offers examples. (Freeze and flight reactions are combined because they overlap in many instances):

WILLFUL REACTIONS

Fight in your mind
Hypervigilance
Silent, ongoing criticism of others
Inflexible thinking, black and white thinking
Frantic defense of opinions
The desperate need to be right
Inflated and arrogant self-image
Manipulative mind
Judgmental mind
Cynicism

Fight in your feelings
Easy to anger
Rage as a way of control
Aggressiveness
Grandiose mood
Constricted withholding of feelings
Fake performance of feelings
Denial of hurt and vulnerability
Restlessness, impatience
Desire to dominate

Fight in your body
Constricted vascular system
Tension headaches
Gastrointestinal distress
Rigid diets, anorexia
Body armoring and stiffness, e.g., neck pain
and low back pain
Forcing your body to exceed limits
(i.e., risk taking, extreme sports)

Fight in your spirit
Religious-based, self-righteous condemnation of others
Spiritual arrogance, having the answers
Dogmatic rigidity
Cynical negation of spirituality

WILL-LESS REACTIONS
Flight in your mind Worrying and ruminating Chronic refusal to decide, maintenance of confusion Inability to think clearly Numbed mind, dissociation Mindlessness Ongoing search for distraction Self-pitying, victimized thinking Automatic people-pleasing Indifference
Flight in your feelings Anxiety, nervousness Helplessness Hopelessness Escape into feelings, overwhelmed Feelings of numbness, frozen
Shame, desire to hide Guilt without having done anything wrong Co-dependence
Flight in your body Wired, anxious sensations Compulsive TV watching Repetitive self-soothing such as excessive masturbation Eating too much, stuffing Avoidance of situations Lack of basic self-care
Flight in your spirit Religious wishful thinking Nondirected spiritual dabbling Emptiness Lack of relatedness to a higher power or larger vision of life Lack of meaning

9. The best way to use the list, above, is to choose one re-action that applies to you. Then you can personalize the information that follows in the next steps.

10. Once you are in fight/flight/freeze, you've entered sur-vival mode. You temporarily can't think clearly. You feel and act convinced that your survival is at stake.

11. The repetition of fight/flight/freeze reactivity in daily life leads to predictable problems. For example:

    • Relationships in which the partners repeatedly trig-ger fight/flight/freeze in each other are miserable. Some break-ups and divorces are acts of mercy, end-ing the pain of living in repetitive states of alarm and distress.

    • Physiologically, fight/flight/freeze is a stressful body state which negatively affects your heart, blood pres-sure, gut, muscles, hormones, breathing. The repeti-tion of these stress states contribute to gastro-intesti-nal distress, low back pain, hypertension, reduction of your immune system's ability to fight off disease, and other stress-involved problems.

    • Emotionally, these reactions can take over your dai-ly life. For example, the suddenness of the rise of anxiety - a racing heart, a light-headed mental state, a tight chest, weak knees, trouble breathing, a feel-ing of dread and foreboding - creates the fear that the anxiety can happen to you again at any time. In this way, anxiety becomes a loop, anxiety breeding more anxiety. You become anxious about becoming anxious.

- Behaviorally, your choices and actions can be badly skewed by the effect of fight/flight/freeze. You can be overly angry when you didn't need to be, you might avoid situations that were really no threat at all, and you can withdraw from opportunities that could have changed the direction of your life.

Sometimes, of course, there is real threat. In those instances, your fight/flight/freeze reactions are crucial for your survival.

12. By using the list in **Step 8**, you can begin to notice and name your patterns of fight/flight/freeze. With this self-knowledge, you can gain some mastery over your reactions.

    For example, you begin to notice that you feel hopeless (a form of emotional flight) after someone criticizes you. With this self-knowledge, choice increases: you can notice your hopeless feeling without treating it as the truth.

13. In Assagioli's words, instead of automatically *identifying* with the reactive pattern, you can learn to notice it, name it and *disidentify* from it (Assagioli, 1965). **Stream of Consciousness** (**Practice 4**) is specifically designed to strengthen this inner skill.

14. Disidentification **is not** the denial of your reactions or feelings. It is the noticing, naming and conscious choice of whether or not to engage with them.

    The husband who notices but does not say out loud the cruel thoughts in his mind, the recovering alcoholic who notices the impulse to drink but distracts herself from it, the student who begins to panic at a test but instead chooses to follow his breath and calm down, are moments in which disidentification makes someone's life better.

    The cruel thoughts, the impulse to drink, the test panic, and many other fight/flight/freeze reactions may rise up in you, but you can choose whether or not to give them energy.

15. Although it is not always possible, the best response to fear-based reactions includes but is more than disidentification. It is adding the element of turning toward your fear with empathy.

    How can you have empathy for your fears? When you grasp that your brain's fear center is only trying to survive, you can treat its productions – worries, warnings, anxiety, fight/flight/freeze - with gratitude for its protective efforts.

16. What forms can empathy take once you have been stimulated by fear?

Here are a few examples:

- Use self-talk in which, in the privacy of your mind, you reassure the fear center that you received its message and you thank it for its efforts on your behalf.
- Follow your breath, e.g., the **Centering** method **(Practice 3),** so that your body calms down.
- Conjure a powerful image in your imagination and ask the image to take the fear away from you. Some people use religious or spiritual images for this purpose.
- Impose rational thinking and force yourself to analyze the actual degree of the threat.
- Use **Let Go (Practice 1)**, repeating it over and over again in your mind, to counteract the fear and calm yourself down.

17. When you practice the inner skills of disidentification and empathy, *three great benefits* begin to flow to you:
    - **Present-moment Awareness**. As your awareness is less absorbed in fear-based reactions, it can focus more on the present moment. This state of mindfulness - being with what is happening - is a way of being happier (Kabat-Zinn, 1991). The increase in your present-moment awareness also improves your focus and memory (Jha et al., 2011).
    - **Physical Restoration**. Your body will not undergo the physiological alarm state as often, thereby reducing the chance of stress-based illness developing.

- **Brain Health**. Repeated acts of awareness and empathy physiologically grow new neurons in the executive center of your brain, which in turn makes you more capable of dealing with the productions of your fear center (Hoelzel et al., 2011).

The Opening of the Personality

18. Your fear center, however, doesn't shut off. You will always have fear-based reactions. Why is this so? Why is the fear center so active, and why does it send out so many worries, warnings and anxieties?

    The answer is that your fear center knows something your conscious mind would prefer to forget. Your brain, though hard-wired to survive, knows that change, loss and death are built into your life. It is constantly perceiving threat because it knows that your life is temporary.

    Philosophers East and West have referred to this fact of life as "the truth of impermanence" and "the human condition." We call it our basic *vulnerability,* a reality shared with every living being.

19. There is no answer *to* your vulnerability. It just is: it is life as life is. There is, however, an answer *in* your vulnerability. In fact, there are two answers.

20. The first answer is *connection.* It is accepting the fact that every living being without exception is vulnerable,

including you. This acceptance increases your feelings of connection and empathy with everyone and everything around you.

Connection and empathy are healthy, pleasurable, touching and rewarding for you. It can lead to a life of loving concern for others, a life in which your own fears become unimportant, even boring.

21. The second answer is *transpersonal.* By willingly accepting your vulnerability and letting go of any self-centered wish that life should be the way you want it to be, you start on the road to finding a way of harmony with life as life is. You delay this important journey if you keep trying to willfully impose your willpower over life or by trying to will-lessly escape the realities of life.

    Transpersonal development posits that you already have in your own deeper nature the resources to be in harmony. The process is one of opening your personality to new discoveries about your deeper resources.

22. The first transpersonal discovery is inner peace. Inner peace includes but goes far beyond relaxation. It is a taste of the serenity of awareness itself when it is freed from absorption in your fear-based patterns.

23. Increasing inner peace creates the conditions for noticing a subtler level of your mind – guiding inner wisdom.

24. This second discovery, guiding inner wisdom, comes to you in words, images, body sensations, energies, emotions, and/or gut knowing, depending on your personal style. You learn to distinguish inner wisdom from all of the other activities of your mind.

25. As a relationship builds with your guiding inner wisdom, you realize that it has a definite orientation – it is trying to lead you toward your life purpose. This urge inside you toward a life of purpose is the same as the natural evolutionary urge in all of nature.

26. It takes time to clarify the vision and form of your life purpose. It must be distinguished from the goals that society has conditioned in you.

    You have something intimate and natural inside you that will help the world, even the world of one other person, and you are supposed to bring it out. It takes courage to act on your life purpose: you can't predict how it will be received or what it will serve. You bring it out in the best way you can, and you let go of the outcome.

27. As you orient around your life purpose, fear fades - even though it is physiologically impossible for it to go away. As your awareness is less caught up in fear, it is liberated more often to be serene in the present moment. In this liberation of awareness, you are creating the conditions for new discoveries and breakthrough experiences.

Moving from Separateness to Oneness

Matter is spirit moving slowly enough for us to

see it. —*TEILHARD DE CHARDIN*

28. Through the systematic refining of your awareness, you can experience a transpersonal aspect of your nature which is beyond your mind and body and therefore does not undergo the change, loss and death of your mind and body. All **Huntington Method** practices are, ultimately, oriented toward this discovery.

29. Transpersonal awareness practices can lead to moments of being in awareness itself. You begin to discover a quietly pervading joy which Assagioli said "…is in the very substance of reality." You unite with it more and more as a daily experience.

30. At times, immersion into awareness itself can be total. It is awareness of awareness, an energy experience of immersion into an infinite field of radiant bliss. Bliss leads to life-changing knowledge.

31. The knowledge is embedded in the bliss itself. In brain research, the state is called "absolute unitary being" (Newberg & D'Aquili, 2001). The mystics call

it "home." In yogic language, they call the experience *satchitananda*: being-wisdom-bliss.

It isn't the wisdom of something intellectual. It is the wisdom of disappearing into the energy of bliss, a state Dante described as "...a light whose glory makes the Creator visible to the created mind."

The discovery brings complete reassurance. The circle is complete: you begin in energy and you end in energy. The essence of your transpersonal self is now known to you.

Assagioli put it this way: "Spiritual realization is the direct experience of the part of your nature which is identical to the great energy pervading the universe."

32. This has nothing to do with belief. This is all verifiable through your direct personal experience.

33. All is well.

34. Obstacles are natural at all of these phases and to be expected along the transpersonal path. The study of these obstacles is necessary to make the path easier.

35. Health professionals are ideally suited to do transpersonal work because they have formally studied human development, psychology, health and illness and can guide people with discernment toward these discoveries.

PART SIX:

A Vision for Transpersonal Development

The Implications of Transpersonal Development

Educating yourself about the real possibilities inherent in transpersonal development has broader implications for your community:

New Training. Helping Professionals (nurses, physicians, counselors, psychologists, clergy, therapists, educators, health and wellness coaches, etc.) learn how to awaken dormant transpersonal resources in their patients, clients, students and employees.

Information. The awareness of transpersonal resources becomes a common understanding, an obvious fact about human nature.

Self-Worth. The dignity of each person is increased by realizing (making real) the fact of their transpersonal resources. This dignity naturally increases a positive and beneficial attitude toward others.

Lifelong Learning. People of any age can learn how to awaken their dormant transpersonal resources. The resulting discoveries have no limit in terms of new experiences and new feelings and can provide an enduring way of positive living.

Meaning. The time and effort given to awakening dormant transpersonal resources is far more interesting and meaningful than the pursuit of leisurely distractions offered by our present culture.

Life Purpose. The purpose of human life, whatever else it may be, is to discover and express what life has given us.

Scientific Research. Research into the most effective ways to awaken dormant transpersonal resources becomes an important topic for both individual and community quality of life.

Spirituality. The inner, hidden realities that mystics, saints, and spiritual teachers have described down through the centuries becomes a real experience for more people.

Universality. The recognition of transpersonal resources in every person without exception offers an additional bond for people beyond cultural differences.

Transpersonal Commentary

William James: Our normal waking consciousness – rational consciousness as we call it – is but one special type of consciousness, whilst all about it, parted from it by the flimsiest of screens, there lie potential forms of consciousness entirely different. We may go through life without suspecting their existence; but apply the requisite stimulus, and at a touch they are there in all their completeness...No account of the universe in its totality can be final which leaves these other forms of consciousness quite disregarded.

Carl Jung: Having consulted with patients from the four corners of the earth, I have come to the conclusion that for anyone over thirty-five years old, their primary problem is not having yet developed a spiritual perspective on life.

Viktor Frankl: During the three years in Auschwitz and Dachau, I decided I was responsible for making use of the slightest chance of survival and ignoring the great danger around me. You see, meaning should be discovered from within...In contrast to religious or philosophical meaning, which can change over time, individual human meaning remains permanent.

Roberto Assagioli: Higher consciousness objectively exists. It is one of the primary experiences of living.

Rumi: I am so small I can barely be seen. How can this great love be inside me?

Ken Wilber: The alarming fact is that any realization of depth carries a terrible burden. Those who are allowed to see are simultaneously saddled with the obligation to communicate that vision in no uncertain terms...only by investing and speaking your vision with passion, can the truth, one way or another, finally penetrate the reluctance of the world…It is your duty to promote that discovery.

Aldous Huxley: Knowledge is a function of being. When there is a change in the knower, there is a change in the nature and amount of knowing.

Carl Jung: He (the Eastern spirituality student) wishes to free himself from nature; in keeping with this aim, he seeks in meditation the condition of egolessness and emptiness. I, on the other hand, wish to persist in the state of living contemplation of nature and of psychic images. I want to be freed neither from human beings, nor from myself, nor from nature; for all these appear to me the greatest of miracles. Nature, the psyche, and life appears to me like divinity unfolded – and what more could I wish for?

Karlfried Durckheim: The individual who is increasingly aware of his own wholeness is part of a general trend. The trend is that people are increasingly resentful of the worldly pressures that functionalize them and reduce them to socioeconomic roles. Their resentment stems not from their personality but from their true nature. When that nature is suppressed, the result is an anguish that therapy focused on performing in the world cannot cure. The only answer is therapy in which true nature is the point.

Dante: The light of God that shines throughout the heavens is lit in us.

Edgar Mitchell: There are no unnatural or supernatural phenomena, only very large gaps in our knowledge of what is natural.

Charles Tart: Because people usually identify with the personal self, which tends to separate us, rather than the transpersonal, which experientially impresses us with our fundamental unity and oneness with each other and life, knowledge of and contact with the transpersonal is of great value in solving the problems of a world divided against itself, including the world of our own self.

George Leonard and Michael Murphy: All of us possess a vast, untapped potential...and there are few tragedies so pervasive, so difficult to justify, as the waste of that potential.

Meister Eckhart: The eye with which I see God is the same eye with which God sees me.

Karlfried Durckheim: A great moment comes when you suddenly see that everything that happens in and around us is a part of Being's effort to manifest itself in space and time. This insight may be accompanied by horrified realization of the extent to which we are preventing it from doing so in our own life. In failing to bring Being to form, we fortunately become aware of the wholeness that Life intends us to have. The more capable we become of understanding Life's purpose, the more suffering if we still cannot accept that purpose and fail to make room for the wave of Being that seeks form in us.

Dante: I see man's mind cannot be satisfied
Unless it be illumined by that Truth
Beyond which there exists no other truth.
Within that Truth, once man's mind reaches it,
It rests like a wild beast within its den.
And it can reach it…!

References

Alcoholics Anonymous (1984). *Pass it on*. New York: AA World Services.

Assagioli, R. (undated notes). Assagioli Archives, Florence, Italy.

Assagioli, R. (1965). *Psychosynthesis*. New York: Penguin Books.

Assagioli, R. (1974). *Act of will*. New York: Viking

Assagioli, R. (1991). *Transpersonal development*. London: HarperCollins.

Austin, J. (2006). *Zen-Brain reflections*. Cambridge MA: MIT Press.

Bauer, R. (2011). The awareness issue. *Transmission: Journal of the Awareness Field*. Press Publisher Online Publishing System.

Benson H. (1975). *The relaxation response*. New York: HarperCollins.

Bible (2001). *English standard version.* Nashville: United Methodist Publishing House

Birnbaum A., Birnbaum, L., & Mayseless, O. (2008). The role of spirituality in mental health. *International Journal of Transpersonal Studies,* Vol. 27.

Brooks, D. (2008). The neural Buddhists. *New York Times.* May 13, 2008

Di Carlo, R. (1996). *Towards a New World View: Conversations at the Leading Edge.* Epic Publishing. www.healthy.net/scr/interview.aspx?Id=199. Retrieved 3/4/12.

Dossey, B. (2010). *Florence Nightingale: Mystic, visionary, healer.* Philadelphia: F.A. Davis.

Dossey, L. (1994). *Healing words: The power of prayer and the practice of medicine.* New York NY: HarperCollins.

Dossey, L. (2009). *The power of premonitions: How knowing the future can shape our lives.* New York NY: Penguin.

Dossey, L. (2013). *The one mind: How our individual mind is part of a greater consciousness, and why it matters.* Carlsbad, CA: Hay House.

Farb, N., Segal, Z., Mayberg, H., Bean, J., McKeon, D.., Fatima, Z. & Anderson, A. (2007). Attending to the present: mindfulness meditation reveals distinct neural modes of self-reference. *Social Cognitive and Affective Neuroscience.*

2(4): 313-322 first published online August 13, doi:10.1093/scan/nsm030

Follman, M. (2012). Personal communication.

Fjorback, L. & Walach, H. (2012). Meditation based therapies - A systematic review and some critical observations. *Religions,* 3(1), 1-18; doi:10.3390/rel3010001. Retrieved July 3, 2012, http://www.mdpi.com/2077-1444/3/1/1

Frankl, V. (1997). *Man's search for meaning.* New York: Pocket Books.

Greeson J. Mindfulness research update: 2008. *Complementary Health Practice. Review,* 2009 Jan; 14(1):0–18.

Grossman, R. (2012). Personal communication.

Hanson, R. (2009). *Buddha's brain: The practical neuroscience of happiness, love and wisdom.* Oakland CA: New Harbinger.

Hoelzel, B.K., Carmody, J., Vangel, M., Congleton, C., Yerramsetti, S.M., Gard, T., & Lazar, S.W. (2011). Mindfulness practice leads to increases in regional brain gray matter density. *Psychiatry Research: Neuroimaging, 191,* 36-43.

Jha, A.P., Stanley, E.A, Kiyonaga, A., Wong, L., & Gelfand, L. (2010). Examining the protective effects of mindfulness training on working memory and affective experience. *Emotion,* 10(1), 54–64.

Kabat-Zinn, J. (1991). *Full catastrophe living: Using the wisdom of your body and mind to face pain, stress and illness*. New York: Bantam Dell.

Kim E.S., Sun J.K., Park N., Kubzansky L.D. & Peterson C. (2012). Purpose in life and reduced risk of myocardial infarction among older U.S. adults with coronary heart disease: A two-year follow-up. *Journal of Behavioral Medicine*, February.

King, M.L. (1993). A Christmas sermon on peace. In D.Wells (Ed.), *We Have a Dream* (pp.288-295). New York: Carroll & Graf.

Kohls N., Sauer S., Offenbächer M., & Giordano J. (2011). Spirituality: an overlooked predictor of placebo effects? *Philosophical Transactions of the Royal Society of London, Series B, Biological Sciences,* June 27; 366(1572):1838-48. Retrieved July 31, 2012.

Lewis, C.S. (1966). *Surprised by joy*. New York: Harcourt, Brace, Jovanovich.

McFarlane, A.C. (2010). The long-term costs of traumatic stress: intertwined physical and psychological consequences. *World Psychiatry*, 9 (1): 3-10.

National Center for Complementary and Alternative Medicine. *Meditation for health purposes - executive summary*. Available at: nccam.nih.gov/news/events/meditation08/ summary.htm. Retrieved 8/30/11.

REFERENCES

Newberg, A. & D'Aquili, E. (2001). *Why God won't go away: Brain science & the biology of belief.* New York NY: Ballantine.

New York Times (2012). *Katherine Russell Rich, 56; Wrote of Battle with Cancer.* Obituary by Margalit Fox, April 7, 2012, p. D7.

Ornish, D. (1990). *Dr. Dean Ornish's program for reversing heart disease.* New York: Ballantine Books.

Penfield, W. (1975). *The mystery of the mind.* Princeton, NJ: Princeton University Press.

Schaub, B., Luck, S. & Dossey, B. (2012). Integrative nurse coaching for health and wellness. *Alternative and Complementary Therapies,* 18 (1), February.

Schaub, B. & Schaub, R. (1997). *Healing addictions: The vulnerability model of recovery.* Albany NY: Delmar.

Schaub, R. (1995). Alternative health and spiritual practices. *Alternative Health Practitioner*, 1(1).

Schaub, R. (1995a). Meditation, adult development and health. *Alternative Health Practitioner*, 1 (3).

Schaub, R. (1996). Meditation, adult development and health: Part two. *Alternative Health Practitioner*, 2 (1).

Schaub, R. & Follman, M. (1996). Meditation, adult development and Health: Part three. *Alternative Health Practitioner*, 2, (3).

Schaub, R. & Schaub, B. (1994). Freedom in jail: Assagioli's notes. *Quest Magazine*, 7, (3), Autumn.

Schaub, R. & Schaub, B. (2003). *Dante's path: A practical approach to achieving inner wisdom.* New York NY: Penguin.

Schaub, R. & Schaub, B. (2009). *The end of fear: A spiritual path for realists.* Carlsbad CA: Hay House, New York.

Seligman, M, Steen, T., Park, N. & Peterson, C. (2005). Positive psychology progress: Empirical validations of interventions. In *American Psychologist.* Washington DC: APA Press.

Shin, L.M. & Liberzon, I. (2010). The neurocircuitry of fear, stress, and anxiety disorders. *Neuropsychopharmacology.* Jan; 35(1):169-91.

Whitmore, J. (2009). *Coaching for performance.* London: Nicholas Brealey

About The Authors

Richard Schaub, PhD, has trained hundreds of health professionals internationally in the clinical applications of meditation, imagery, and transpersonal psychology. His recent teaching includes Veterans Adminstration hospital staff, Federal Emergency Management counselors, and Wall Street employees. His own formal meditation training, starting in 1971, includes Zen, mindfulness, psychosynthesis, Catholic visualization practices, and QiGong.

He is director of the Huntington Meditation and Imagery Center and the New York Psychosynthesis Institute and guest faculty of the International Nurse Coach Association and the Istituto di Psicosintesi, Florence, Italy. His previous books, co-authored with his wife, Bonney, are *Healing Addictions: The Vulnerability Model of Recovery; Dante's Path: A Practical Approach to Achieving Inner Wisdom*, and *The End of Fear: A Spiritual Path for Realists.* His next book, *The Classic Spiritual Path,* will be available in the Fall, 2013.

He is a state-licensed psychotherapist who leads meditation and transpersonal development groups in Huntington, New

York. Prior to private practice, he worked in psychiatric re-habilitation, alcohol halfway houses, cardiac and cancer re-habilitation, directed an adolescent day hospital program, and supervised graduate counseling students at Hofstra University and St. John's University.

He can be reached via his website: www.huntingtonmeditation.com

Bonney Gulino Schaub, RN, MS, PMHCNS-BC, is co-director and core faculty of the International Nurse Coach Association and the Integrative Nurse Coach Certificate Program (www.inursecoach.com). She is also co-director of the Huntington Meditation and Imagery Center.

After working in medical-surgical nursing and in-patient psy-chiatry, she worked as a detox coordinator and nurse psycho-therapist in an alcohol and drug treatment program. She sub-sequently formulated the *Vulnerability Model of Recovery*, a model of emotional and spiritual development that has been adapted by drug and alcohol treatment centers in the United States, Canada, and Italy.

In addition to books co-authored with her husband, Richard, she has written chapters on addictions counseling and clini-cal imagery for the standard textbook in the field, *Holistic Nursing: A Handbook for Practice, 6ᵗʰ Edition.* Her work was featured in Oprah's **O** Magazine and was a finalist in the National Books for a Better Life awards. Her next book, co-authored with Barbara Dossey and Susan Luck, will be *Integrative Nurse Coaching in Health and Wellness*.

Together, Bonney and Richard have been lifelong seekers of knowledge. In addition to four years of postgraduate training and certification in the transpersonal psychology of psychosynthesis, they studied brain-wave biofeedback at the Menninger Foundation lab of Elmer Green and were QiGong students of Dr. Ching Tse Lee. They have traveled extensively to deepen their understanding of the healing principles in the various spiritual traditions. Their studies led to the monastery of the Medieval mystic, Hildegard of Bingen, in Germany, and to the Sufi Rumi's Mevlevi Order in Istanbul. They created and led several sacred art and visualization retreats to Florence, Italy. Their teaching is enriched by such cross-cultural influences.

Index

Made in the USA
San Bernardino, CA
27 March 2014